D0103798

HAIG

MILITARY PROFILES
SERIES EDITOR
Dennis E. Showalter, Ph.D.
Colorado College

*Instructive summaries for general and expert
readers alike, volumes in the Military Profiles
series are essential treatments of significant and
popular military figures drawn from world history,
ancient times through the present.*

HAIG

The Evolution of a Commander

Andrew A. Wiest

Potomac Books, Inc.
Washington, D.C.

Library of Congress Cataloging-in-Publication Data

Wiest, Andrew A.
   Haig : the evolution of a commander / Andrew A. Wiest.— 1st ed.
      p. cm.—(Military profiles)
   Includes bibliographical references and index.
   ISBN 1-57488-683-5 (acid-free paper)—ISBN 1-57488-684-3
(pbk. : acid-free paper)
      1. Haig, Douglas, Sir, 1861–1928.   2. Generals—Great Britain—
   Biography.   3. World War, 1914–1918—Campaigns.   I. Title.
   II. Series.

   DA69.3H3W54 2005
   940.4'0092—dc22   2005009810

Printed in the United States of America on acid-free paper that meets the American National Standards Institute z39-48 Standard.

Potomac Books, Inc.
22841 Quicksilver Drive
Dulles, Virginia 20166

FIRST EDITION

10 9 8 7 6 5 4 3 2 1

Contents

Maps

Preface

A cursory tour of the "military history" shelves of any major bookstore in the United States reveals a continued national fascination with World War II. It was a time in which giants strode the world stage—players of both mythic good and terrible evil. It was a war of sweeping drama in which the fate of the world seemed to hinge on single decisions or indeed the actions of individual soldiers. It was the war of the "greatest generation" and the "band of brothers." Interested readers, though, must search diligently to find the location of books concerning World War I, often tucked away behind more salable tomes. In the mind of the book-buying American public the Great War pales in comparison to its younger sibling. World War I was slow moving, and, though it was tragic, it was rather too dull to seize the American imagination. The protagonists of the conflict seem bumbling and out of their depth rather than either heroic or evil. Perhaps the lack of written attention is due to the state of communications technology that existed at the time of the respective conflicts. Film footage of the Great War seems herky-jerky and almost comic as soldiers silently rush by—reminding the viewer perhaps of Charlie Chaplin. For whatever reason, though, World War I has receded into the realm of the nearly forgotten distant past—a murky realm of myths and half-truths.

Americans can be forgiven their relative ignorance of the Great War, for it was hardly an American war at all—with U.S. soldiers entering combat only near the end of the conflict. For Europeans, though, the war and its agonies formed the most critical series of events of the twentieth century. In the case of Britain the Great War was the cause of more sacrifice and death than World War II and was the only occasion in history that the island nation chose to raise a mass army to face the leading continental power in land combat. Though bookshelves in London carry a wider assortment of Great War titles, the British public has developed its own, rather unique, mythological dogma regarding World War I and its consequences. To most Britons the Great War represents the nadir of the Edwardian military. The chief commanders of the conflict were hidebound relics of a bygone age—turn-of-the-century gentlemen amateurs, trained in the army of the Raj and unable to come to grips with the first truly modern war. British soldiers, volunteers and the flower of their generation, fought heroically at the behest of their unthinking leaders and were needlessly sacrificed in the soulless trenches and bottomless mud of Flanders. Even through five years of combat the British high command apparently learned nothing—achieving final, and questionable, victory through luck alone.

Within the field of military history, though, the nature of the Great War is the subject of continuing, often acrimonious, debate. Usually staid historians sometimes very nearly come to blows in discussions involving World War I. The historian protagonists of the argument represent two diametrically opposing viewpoints. There exists a powerful traditional school of thought concerning World War I that informs the public perception of the conflict. Born in part during a postwar publication flurry of memoirs and biographies, the traditionalist school came of age in the wake of World War II and flowered fully in the Vietnam era.[1] At least in part informed by the events of their own time, traditionalist historians contend that the British high command was little better than a collection of murderers—sending their men to their doom in endless lines. At the furthest extreme, the polemic title of John Laffin's *British Butchers and Bunglers of World War One* does not even require the reader to open the book to discern its contents.

A new group of revisionist historians, however, has emerged to challenge the traditionalist view. While not totally exonerating the British high command of its grievous errors, the revisionist school has endeavored to look beneath the surface veneer of British failure and has discovered a rich new vein of historical enquiry. The revisionists, led by the late John Terraine, along with Gary Sheffield and Paddy Griffith, agree that the British army and its command structure were at best flawed instruments at the outset of the Great War, leading to the apparent disasters of the Somme and Passchendaele. However, far from learning nothing from their mistakes, the British army experienced a steep "learning curve" in the first years of the conflict. As a result, by 1918 the British Expeditionary Force (BEF) was the most potent army in the field, even laying waste to the vaunted German army in a series of nearly forgotten battles termed "The Hundred Days."

Thus, unlike nearly any other subject area, there exists a great divide in historical perceptions of World War I. To most, World War I represents needless slaughter at the hands of murderous commanders. Within the field of Great War history, though, the revisionists presently hold sway and contend that the commanders of the BEF achieved the greatest single military victory ever in British history and wrought a sea change in modern military thought. As might be expected with such stark, opposing viewpoints attacks across the historical divide have been numerous and vitriolic. Thus a great storm swirls around World War I history, a storm that quite naturally has centered on the person of the commander in chief of the BEF: Sir Douglas Haig.

Though many of his decisions and actions were controversial during his tenure at the head of the BEF, after the Great War Haig became a revered, almost fatherly figure, to the British public. His death in 1928 sparked a national wave of mourning, and his funeral attracted as many mourners as did that of Winston Churchill some thirty-five years later.[2] In the intervening years, though, the public perception of Haig has altered, transforming the field marshal into a murderous, semi-barbaric figure. Indeed, public pronouncements concerning Haig now drip with venom usually reserved for only the worst war criminals.

On the occasion of the eightieth anniversary of the armistice a national British newspaper, the *Express*, ran a story on Haig under the headline, "He led a million men to their deaths," and later went on to assert that the men had died needlessly as the sole result of his orders. The paper even launched a campaign to remove Haig's statue from Whitehall because its close proximity to the monument to Britain's war dead, the Cenotaph, sullied the memory of the glorious fallen.[3] Perhaps, though, the best indicator of the public perception of Haig can be seen in his portrayal in the satirical British television series *Blackadder Goes Forth*. The series pillories British commanders as inept at best and insane at worst—sacrificing the lives of their men for inches of tortured ground. Haig appears only in a short clip in which he sweeps toy soldiers from a model of the western front into a dustpan and tosses them away without a second thought.

In the historical profession more ink has probably been spilled over Haig than over all of the other commanders of World War I combined. Though almost unknown to many in the United States, a historical debate has raged in the United Kingdom over Haig and his leadership of Britain's greatest-ever military effort. Though many of the initial books dealing with Haig were sympathetic biographies written by compatriots, the mood of Great War literature quickly changed. The traditional school has quite successfully portrayed Haig as a chronically mistaken, overly ambitious man who, surrounded by sycophants, consistently believed that God was leading his hand. The frightening combination of Haig's personal traits led to unmitigated disaster. Failing to understand the war, Haig continued to order senseless assaults, and his toadies in General Headquarters (GHQ) were too weak to stand against his wishes. Though the bodies piled higher Haig, who never visited the front to witness the horror of the trenches, stubbornly stuck to his misguided plans, certain of God's favor. In the end only the selfless sacrifice of the brave British soldiery, America's belated entry into the conflict, and Germany's internal collapse allowed a befuddled Haig to achieve a measure of victory. Historian Denis Winter even contends that Haig's deleterious effect on the war did not end in 1918. Supposedly Haig even went so far as to falsify his own diary in an attempt to exonerate himself from his crimes against his nation, thus forever skewing the field of Great War history.[4]

The revisionist field of Great War history began in many ways with John Terraine's 1963 publication of *Douglas Haig: The Educated Soldier*. While paying very close attention to Haig, Terraine devoted much of his work to the nature of the war that surrounded the BEF. What emerged was not a caricature of an over-matched yet overconfident butcher,[5] but a portrait of a thoughtful man who struggled against the insoluble problems posed by trench warfare in the early twentieth century. Taking the challenge issued by Terraine, revisionist historians began to unravel the mysteries of the Great War, contending that the BEF not only met but surmounted the awesome challenge and in so doing altered the nature of future combat. Much of the succeeding revisionist work also centers on Haig, but the conclusions regarding his role in the evolution of the BEF are often at odds. Some revisionists claim that Haig and GHQ were needless impediments to innovation and that the changes in the BEF and its method of war took place in spite of Haig's interference. Others, while acknowledging Haig's mistakes, contend that he learned the craft of a commander in chief well and was indeed the source of much of the innovation to be found in the BEF.

It is quite safe to say that Sir Douglas Haig is the most controversial figure in British military history. Haig far outstrips his nearest competitor, Field Marshal Sir Bernard Montgomery, the flawed victor of El Alamein in World War II. Though "Monty" certainly has his detractors, none have gone so far as to suggest the destruction of his statue in front of the Ministry of Defence in Whitehall. The passion engendered by the continuing arguments over the career of Sir Douglas Haig, though, know no such bounds. To most of the public Haig is a villain—the man who needlessly caused the death of an entire generation of Britain's best and brightest. To the traditionalist historians Haig is at worst a "butcher" or a "donkey." At his best Haig is an arrogant, self-serving general who was unable to realize that he was out of his depth during the Great War. On the other hand the most extreme revisionists claim that Haig was a truly great commander, who helped to alter the very nature of modern warfare. Others, though they recognize Haig's flaws, agree that revolutionary changes were made under his tenure as commander in chief of the BEF. The gulf between the differing historical views on Sir Douglas Haig is truly great, and indeed no other commander in history is the subject of such a wide disparity of opinion. Haig could be anything from the savior of Britain to the butcher of the BEF.

Though fascinating, the historiographical battles over Haig's command have done a disservice to the history of the Great War. So much attention has been lavished on Haig that other, more fruitful, areas of Great War research have been ignored. The historical team of Robin Prior and Trevor Wilson has even called for something of a moratorium on books devoted to Haig, for attention fixated on him has in their view helped "to preserve historical writing about the Great War in its ridiculously protracted adolescence."[6] Even so, Haig remains central to the story of the transformation of the BEF in the Great War, and to the story of the war itself. In recent years Great War history has moved out of its extended adolescence and toward maturity. Seminal works, by both traditionalists and revisionists, have appeared, fundamentally altering the historical perceptions of World War I and its place in history. However, these works have made little impression upon the public mindset regarding the war, and they have received little notice outside a small circle of historians in the United States. It is, then, the purpose of the present study to chronicle and assess the career of Sir Douglas Haig in the light of the important historical work of the past few years. Not intended to be an exhaustive study, the present work introduces readers both to Haig and to the new history surrounding his war. Haig's life will serve as a focus—a lens through which to view the transformation of the Great War.

During my years of study of the Great War I have accumulated several historical debts that should be repaid in part at this point. I first and foremost owe much to my mentor Bentley Brinkerhoff Gilbert for placing me on and then guiding me down the road of study of the Great War. Later in my career, as part of the British Studies Program at the University of Southern Mississippi, I had the chance to return to London each year to renew acquaintance with many of the most influential scholars in the field—affectionately dubbed the "World War I Mafia." At the risk of slighting some of my friends I will single a few out for thanks for their continued help: the late John Terraine, Brian Bond, Pete Simkins, Chris McCarthy, Paddy Griffith, Sean McKnight, Niall Barr, and Paul Harris. Special thanks are due to my friend and colleague Gary Sheffield, who kindly read and offered thoughtful comment on the book in manuscript form. I also wish to thank the War Studies Department at Royal Military Academy Sandhurst and Matt Midlane, the late John Pimlott, and Duncan Anderson for my teaching stint there, which also served as one of the most intense learning experiences of my life. Thanks are also due to the British Commission for Military History for allowing a Yank to join and for serving as such a wonderful sounding board for the field of Great War history. This book would not have been possible without the continued support of the History Department at the University of Southern Mississippi and its chair (and my basketball tormentor) Charles Bolton. It is the generosity of the department that made the pictures in this book possible. I would also like to thank Skeeter Dixon and Don Green from the Department of Geography at the University of Southern Mississippi for kindly producing the maps for this volume. I would also like to thank our departmental secretary Shelia Smith for helping me through this project and for being my friend. Finally, I dedicate this book to my loving wife Jill and our beautiful children Abigail and Luke—all of whom cheerfully put up with being abandoned while I bang away on the computer.

Chronology

1861	Douglas Haig born in Edinburgh, June 19.
1883	Enters the Royal Military College Sandhurst.
1885	Joins the Seventh (Queen's Own) Hussars and sees service in India.
1896	Enters Staff College.
1898	Seconded to the Egyptian Army and sees service in the Sudan Campaign.
1899	Serves under Sir John French as Staff Officer in the Cavalry Division in the Boer War.
1901	Appointed commander of the Seventeenth Lancers.
1903	Appointed Inspector General of Cavalry in India
1905	Marries Dorothy Vivian.
1906	Appointed Director of Military Training at the War Office.
1909	Returns to India as Chief of the General Staff.
1911	Takes over the Aldershot Command.
1914	British declaration of war, Battle of Mons, August. First Battle of Ypres, October–November. Takes command of First Army, December.
1915	Battle of Neuve Chapelle, March. Battle of Aubers Ridge, Battle of Festubert, May. Battle of Loos, September. Takes over as commander in chief of the British Expeditionary Force, December.
1916	Battle of Verdun, February–December. Opening of the Battle of the Somme, July 1. First battlefield use of the tank, September 15. Close of the Battle of the Somme, November.

1917   Calais Conference, February. Opening of the Battle of Arras, April. Failure of the Nivelle Offensive and French Army Mutiny, April–May. Battle of Messines, June. Third Battle of Ypres begins, July 31. Plumer takes over command of the second phase of the Third Battle of Ypres, August. Passchendaele falls, the Third Battle of Ypres ends, November. Battle of Cambrai, November–December.

1918   German offensive opens on the western front, Allied creation of a Supreme Command, March. Battle of Amiens, August. The Hundred Days, August–November. Armistice, November.

1919   Takes command of the Home Forces, April. Haig is created an Earl, August.

1920   Haig retires from active military life.

1921   Formation of the British Legion.

1928   Haig dies, January 29.

HAIG

Chapter 1

The Military Education of Douglas Haig

Douglas Haig was born in Edinburgh, Scotland, on June 19, 1861, the son of John and Rachel Haig who prospered in the whiskey industry and claimed distant relation to the gentility of the main family line. The youngest son of nine surviving children, Douglas Haig was little influenced by his father, who died in 1878. Instead his mother and his sister Henrietta were the prime forces of his young life. The Haig household was strict and regimented, instilling a true sense of discipline in the lad, but also leading him toward a history of personal isolation. Seemingly everything around Douglas Haig served as a reminder of duty and place, including his toy drum with the inscription, "Douglas Haig—sometimes a good boy."[1] A rather indifferent student, Haig first attended school at Clifton and then went on to Brasenose College, Oxford. University life, though, failed to seize the imagination of young Haig, who paid scant attention to his studies. Haig did, however, become increasingly engaged in the university social life of the era, taking on the trappings of a Victorian gentleman.[2] In part because of an intense shyness and a singular lack of communication ability, though, Haig made few lasting friends and remained intentionally aloof and alone. Until the end of his days Haig would remain ill at ease in public and inept in speaking to all but his very few close associates, and as a result he would be branded as snobbish and secretive by those who were better suited to life in the public eye. In later years some historians would interpret Haig's reserved behavior and difficulty in public speaking as symptoms of either a scheming individuality or sheer idiocy.

After a short and undistinguished stay at Oxford, in 1883 Haig took his sister Henrietta's advice and embarked on a career in the military by entering the Royal Military College Sandhurst. Though he was older than most of his classmates, Haig was quite determined to succeed in his chosen career path. When asked to join in on an evening gambling session Haig remarked, "It's all very well for you fellows, you are going into the Army to play at soldiering, I am going in it as a profession and I am going to do well in it."[3] Graduating first in the order of merit Haig received a commission in the Seventh Hussars. A fine rider and polo player, Haig would forever be associated with the cavalry, and before the Great War he would be one of the staunchest defenders of the cavalry's utility in modern war. The charge that Haig remained fixated by the cavalry even after its usefulness had passed remains a central tenet of the traditionalist school of thought regarding Britain and the Great War.[4]

After a brief stint with the Seventh Hussars in India, Haig returned to Britain and worked further to codify cavalry technique. Very ambitious and sure of his own abilities, Haig then entered Staff College, which represented the fast track to promotion. As he had at Sandhurst, Haig excelled, remaining wedded to his studies and aloof from most of his contemporaries. Haig's tenure at Staff College was critical to the formulation of his understanding of the nature of modern war. He learned well that a major conflict would consist of four phases: maneuver, first clash of battle, a wearing-out fight of varying duration, and finally a decisive blow followed by exploitation. Haig, along with the commanders of every combatant nation, certainly expected this model to hold true at the outset of the Great War. Haig also learned that wars would be mobile and that superior morale, not superior firepower, would bring victory to forces that were rather evenly matched. Several historians, led by Tim Travers, argue that Haig learned his lessons so well that he never deviated from their path during World War I as he vainly searched for a decisive battle and an exploitation opportunity for his beloved cavalry.[5]

After Staff College Haig saw brief action in the Sudan before moving on to more significant service in the Boer War. In the difficult struggle that would point out so many of Britain's military failings, General Sir John French served as commander of the British Cavalry Division in South Africa, and Haig served as his chief staff officer. Haig landed the plum position shortly after having lent French 2,500 pounds to avoid bankruptcy. Though some see the timing of the two events as no coincidence and believe that Haig was able to use the debt as leverage for an entire decade,[6] the two officers remained rather close and devoted to the cause of the cavalry. Shortly after arriving in Cape Colony French and Haig took part in the confused Battle of Elandslaagte. In the campaigning that followed Haig played his role well, but he longed for his own command. He received his chance in early 1902 by leading a mobile column engaged in chasing the elusive Boers, and later took over command of the Seventeenth Lancers.

His battlefield experiences in South Africa proved formative for Haig. The British military, lacking a true general staff system, had initially performed poorly. Realizing the need for change, Haig would, in time, become a leading reformer. Haig also learned of the value of machine guns in combat, commenting often on their indispensability and of the need for more such weapons. His appreciation of the machine gun is important, for it is a leading tenet of the traditionalist school that Haig misunderstood and undervalued its use and centrality to the Great War.[7] Haig, though, remained mostly concerned with the future of his beloved cavalry, because some leading figures, including Lord Roberts, contended that the British experience in South Africa indicated that cavalry would best be used in combat as mounted infantry. However, Haig's continuing experience caused him to believe that cavalry could persevere in its more traditional roles of fighting on horseback and exploitation. Even so Haig remained quite certain to train cavalry under his command for both mounted and dismounted combat. As a result the British cavalry was the best such force in the field in the Great War and was able to play an important dual combat role.[8]

Haig, now a leading cavalry theorist, returned to Edinburgh for a brief stint in regimental command, and became aide de camp to King Edward VII. From this point on Haig would enjoy a rather close relationship with Edward and his successor King George V. Certainly Haig had made the proper social connections for advancement, connections he would work hard to cultivate and broaden. His record having caught the attention of General Sir Horatio Kitchener, the commander in chief in India, Haig soon departed Britain to take over the post of Inspector General of Cavalry in India, charged with the training and modernization of the cavalry of the subcontinent.

Perhaps the most meaningful event in Haig's life during this time was personal, not military. On leave in Britain in 1905, Haig met Dorothy Vivian, one of Queen Alexandra's maids of honor. Haig had never spared much time for social niceties or relations with women. However, at age forty-four he found himself quite taken with Dorothy Vivian. Their courtship was something of a whirlwind—engaged within a week and married in Buckingham Palace within a month of their first meeting. The circumstances of the wedding were so rushed that some historians argue that the marriage was only a practical and quite calculated social move for the ambitious officer. Haig's closest associates, though, contend that the marriage brought him completeness and provided the aloof loner with an important and trusted confidant.[9] Haig's own diary entries indicate a considerable warmth of feeling for his wife and support the conclusion that their marriage was truly a lasting union of deep devotion.

While Haig served abroad in India, momentous events were taking place in Britain. The poor performance of the military during the Boer War caused Britain to pause and take stock of the organization of its armed forces. Beginning with the investigation of the Esher Committee into the nature of the War Office, it quickly became apparent that the organization of the British military was far behind the times, and needed an immediate and drastic overhaul. Matters came to a head in 1906 with the election victory of the reform-minded Liberal Party. As a result, Richard Haldane took over as the new Secretary of State for War with a mandate to modernize the British military. Though the nature of a modernized military quickly became apparent to Haldane, he needed aid in translating his ambitious schemes into reality. In April 1906 Haldane recalled Haig from India to the War Office as Director of Military Training. In that post Haig would have considerable influence over arguably the greatest series of military reforms in British history.

With Haig serving as his "right-hand man" Haldane first went about the construction of the British Expeditionary Force (BEF). The War Office concluded that in time of continental war Britain would send a force of six infantry divisions and one cavalry division to France, a total of 120,000 men. Haig and others at the War Office worked out the eventual composition of the BEF, even down to the railway timetables for its journey to the continent. Next Haldane moved on to the more difficult issue of enlarging the British army and making it part of the nation as a whole, a concept rather foreign to Britons more used to a small military that functioned in many ways as a colonial police force. In essence the scheme called for a total of fourteen volunteer territorial divisions to replace the rather motley collections of militia and yeomanry units in the country. The territorial divisions would be trained and staffed on the pattern of the Regular Army, replacing regular units in home defense. Only this innovation would make it possible for Britain to send the BEF to the continent at the outset of war.

Finally, under Haldane the British military moved toward the implementation of a modern General Staff. With his valuable experience Haig once again proved important in the development of the Imperial General Staff, the military body that would find itself charged with prosecuting the Great War. Indeed the creation of the BEF, the Territorial Force, and the Imperial General Staff proved critical to Britain's ability to even play any role in the Great War, much less a decisive role. In the main, credit for these important innovations must fall to Haldane. However, Haig also played a critical role in the process, proving to be a forward-thinking military figure. Though others would work to perfect the new system, Haig was instrumental in its earliest inception and thus instrumental to Britain's military success. In total Haig served at the War Office for four years, a compressed period of innovation and construction. Haldane remarked that, "Haig had a first-rate General Staff mind. When he arrived in London he grasped the situation completely and gave invaluable guidance in the fashioning of both Regular first line and the Territorial second line."[10]

Marked as one of the rising young stars of the British army, in 1909 Haig departed the War Office and returned to India as Chief of the General Staff. His role now centered on taking the Haldane reforms and transforming them into physical reality in the chaotic Indian command system. Haig again achieved considerable success, paring down the staff system in India into a more workable model. In addition he worked hard to prepare forces on the subcontinent for service in a possible war in Europe, and he educated his staff officers regarding possible scenarios of battle against German forces in France. His actions not only suggest that Haig had discerned the opponent in the next conflict, but also that the conflict would be long enough to require the use of Indian forces in Europe. Such thinking was anathema to most military men of the time, who argued that the coming conflict would be short and decisive. In addition there was a powerful inertia against using Indian forces outside the subcontinent. Even so, Haig had made certain that Indian forces were ready, and indeed an Indian Corps came to Britain's call in late 1914, helping to make good the horrific losses of the BEF.

Haig learned much from his continued staff work in India. His summary of the tactical exercise of 1911 deserves special attention as indicative of his military thinking as war neared. He stated:

> No plan of operations can with any safety include more than the first collision with the enemy's force. . . . Plans aiming far beyond the strategical deployment and first collision have been submitted. Such speculations may become harmful if they are allowed to hamper the judgment as the campaign progresses, and to impede initiative. Commanders in war have been known to become so imbued with an idea as never to think of any other contingency; and what we wish for we like to hope and believe.

Haig also remarked on the supposed lack of a British battle doctrine. While the Germans preached envelopment and the French spoke of penetration, Britain seemed to have no sure plan in case of war. Haig argued that such a statement of doctrine would be too limiting and artificial and that the British system was more supple, allowing for a myriad of reactions to a given situation.[11]

Thus in many ways the state of Haig's military thinking upon the outbreak of war is rather difficult to assess. Without doubt he believed both that the offensive was the stronger form of war and that decisive battle was possible, though the tiny BEF would play but a small role in such a confrontation. Haig also certainly believed that the war would follow a set pattern that would result in cavalry aiding in exploitation of a decisive victory. However, Haig was not mindless in his support of the so-called "Cult of the Offensive" that so dominated the militaries of both France and Germany. He argued that the newly modernized BEF had to remain unfettered in its thinking and doctrine, ready to seize and act upon any opportunity that appeared as the coming war unfolded. Thus Haig's thinking was a rather odd mixture of the traditional and the modern. Like the other leading figures of World War I, Haig would find the continuing transition to modern war, though, rather difficult.

In 1911 Haldane recalled Haig from India to take over the prestigious Aldershot Command. In his new position Haig commanded the First and Second Infantry Divisions and the First Cavalry Brigade—the only true army corps in the British Empire. As an outsider from India Haig experienced some initial difficulties in leading the most important command in Britain, especially since he was only fifty and had been selected for the position over several more senior generals. Haig's main role now centered around the training of what would become I Corps of the BEF. In that task he succeeded admirably. Though at the outset of war the BEF was small, it was quite possibly the best trained army in the field, able to fend off much larger German forces at both Mons and First Ypres. Haig's work under Haldane and now at Aldershot was, thus, critical first to the avoidance of disaster and then to achieving ultimate victory.

Haig's time at Aldershot brought out both the best and worst of his character. Though he remained quite reserved, contemporaries noticed a mellowing in Haig's character at this point, and he was able to elicit the unquestioning support of his officers and men. However, Haig again proved unable to master the political aspects of command, and his inability to communicate remained quite apparent. It was so bad that one of his subordinates later referred to Haig as, "the most inarticulate man I have ever met."[12] Shy and bumbling in public, Haig earned the ire of professional politicians who he in turn viewed as both meddlesome and tiresome. In the main his relations with politicians would remain sour throughout the Great War and would contribute to a costly series of clashes—most notably with David Lloyd George.

By the time war clouds began to gather in 1914 Haig had very nearly reached the pinnacle of British command. His views were, in the main, standard for most of his generation. War had a definite nature and would conform to a series of set rules. On this point historians agree—Douglas Haig entered the Great War, as did all other commanders, expecting to fight a conflict that conformed to past norms. However, World War I would in fact become the first modern, industrialized, total war. As such the conflict would shatter all accepted rules of warfare, leaving outmatched commanders forced to improvise and extemporize a new doctrine. It is on this point that historians differ. Did Douglas Haig succeed in facing the new challenge and help to alter war as he had helped to alter the British military? Or was Douglas Haig an inarticulate and repressive obstacle to innovation who succeeded only by accident?

Chapter 2

A Corps Commander Rises to Prominence

WHILE HAIG WAS IN COMMAND at Aldershot momentous events inexorably drew a distracted Great Britain toward the cataclysm of World War I. At home Britain struggled through a period of constitutional crisis and reform, leading to the eventual passage of a controversial Home Rule Bill for Ireland. The issue that had so plagued Britain for years, though, was not destined for such an easy solution. In Ireland civil war threatened as forces both in the Protestant North and in the Catholic South armed to fight over the impending implementation of home rule. The crisis quickly escalated and led to a confused series of events in 1914 known as the Curragh Mutiny, in which several leading military figures indicated that they would not obey a governmental order to coerce Ulster. For his part Haig remained studiously neutral during the crisis, but the possibility of civil war in Ireland did much to distract the government of Herbert Asquith, the Prime Minister, at a pivotal time in world history—so much so that the events drawing

Europe to war did not become the subject of governmental focus until July, nearly a month after the assassination of Austrian Archduke Francis Ferdinand in Sarajevo.

In the years since the ascension of Kaiser Wilhelm II to the throne of the German Empire in 1888, a series of German diplomatic blunders had slowly driven Britain into the arms of its hereditary enemy France. By 1904, in part because of an escalating naval race with Germany, the British and French had signed the *Entente Cordiale.* An ensuing series of German and French clashes over Morocco then served to harden the friendly agreement into a de facto military alliance, though the British government continued to treasure the illusion of choice in the matter of war. By 1914, though, even the majority of the more pacifistic members of the Asquith government had come to the conclusion that Britain would have to aid France in the case of any German invasion. Nearly all politicians and military men alike believed that alone France would certainly lose such a conflict, as in 1870, leading to a German domination of the continent of Europe and a consequent threat to the very existence of the British Empire.

British fears became reality upon the German invasion of France. Having long feared the coming of war, the continental powers each stood ready, confident and secure in their detailed military planning. The French relied on Plan 17, a direct and rather unsubtle assault into Alsace-Lorraine. On the other hand, Germany's vaunted Schlieffen Plan called for an encirclement of the French forces in Alsace-Lorraine prosecuted by armies wheeling into France from the north. Though ingenious, the German plan proved logistically unsound and made it impossible to win the ultimate victory. Britain, however, had undertaken nothing more than a series of staff talks regarding possible military actions to aid France in case of war. Thus Britain was in many ways in the worst possible situation, committed to war but with no true military plan for the conflict. As a result, as the Asquith government moved to declare war upon Germany it also called together Asquith's leading military advisors, including Haig, to extemporize a plan for war.

The scheme that had resulted from the staff talks, largely developed by General Henry Wilson, called for the BEF to rush to France and detrain at Maubeuge. After forming up the BEF would then join the left (northern) flank of the French lines near the city of Mons in Belgium. While the French attained glorious victory further south adhering to the dictates of Plan 17, the BEF would be relegated to the rather mundane duty of serving as a flank guard. The existence of such a plan, though, came as a surprise to many within the British military. Field Marshal Sir John French, elevated to command of the BEF, advocated altering the plan and landing the BEF on the coast at Antwerp to cooperate with the Belgians in threatening the German right flank. Though operations on the Belgian coast would always remain something of a fixation for French,[1] his plan was rejected, but with war at hand British planning remarkably remained undecided.

When it came Haig's turn to speak, he came out against the Antwerp scheme, questioning the ability of the tiny BEF to survive virtually alone against sustained German assault in such a situation. Haig then went on to make several points to the assembled military and political leaders, which deserve to be quoted at length to demonstrate his military thinking at the dawn of the Great War.

> 1st That Great Britain and Germany would be fighting for their existence. Therefore the war was bound to be a long war, and neither would acknowledge defeat after a short struggle . . . I held that we must organise our resources *for a war of several years.* 2nd Great Britain must at once take in hand the creation of an Army. I mentioned one million as the number to aim at immediately, remarking that that was the strength originally proposed for the Territorial Force by Lord Haldane. Above all, we ought to aim at having a strong and effective force when we came to discuss peace at a Conference of the Great Powers. 3rd We only had a small number of trained officers and N.C.O.s. These must be economised. The need for efficient instructors would become at once apparent. I urged that a considerable proportion of officers and N.C.O.s should be withdrawn forthwith from the Expeditionary Force. . . . Lastly, my

advice was to send as strong an Expeditionary Force as possible, and as soon as possible, to join the French Forces and to arrange to increase that force as rapidly as possible.[2]

Thus it becomes apparent that Haig's advice was critical in the decision for the BEF to stand on the French left flank, where its presence would play a crucial role in the coming struggle. Also, while most military leaders in Europe prophesied a short, decisive conflict, Haig realized that the war would quite likely be long and difficult. Long enough indeed for Britain to raise and equip a mass army for the first time in its history.

Within days the structure of the British wartime military was set, with the irascible Field Marshal Sir Kitchener installed as Secretary of State for War, French as the commander in chief of the BEF and Haig as commander of I Corps. Kitchener affirmed the plan to stand on the French left flank, and more importantly chose to create a new volunteer army rather than rely upon the proven territorial scheme. Both decisions caused Haig great worry. Haig believed that the creation of the so-called "Kitchener Army" would result in grave training deficiencies, leaving the units at a distinct disadvantage against their German foes. Regarding the military plan, Haig hoped that the tiny BEF would not be wasted in battle before it had a chance even to absorb its reserve components.

Of greatest importance, though, was the troubled command dynamic that quickly beset the BEF. The relationship between French and Kitchener was strained and contentious from the start.[3] French was quite concerned that Kitchener, the most famous soldier in the Empire, would attempt to assert his own personal command over the BEF. For his part Kitchener had grave doubts concerning French's ability and temperament. The doubts and suspicions that existed between the two men placed great strain on the leadership structure of the BEF, and would be exacerbated in times of trouble.

Though thrilled to find himself in command of I Corps, and determined to do his duty as a loyal subordinate, Haig also had doubts concerning French's command abilities. On August 11, on the occasion of a royal inspection of the Aldershot Command, King George V asked Haig his opinion of French:

> I told him at once, as I felt it my duty to do so, that from my experience with Sir John in the South African War, he was certain to do his utmost loyally to carry out any orders which the Government might give him. I had grave doubts, however, whether either his temper was sufficiently even or his military knowledge sufficiently thorough to enable him to discharge properly the very difficult duties which will devolve upon him during the coming operations with Allies on the Continent. In my own heart, I know that French is quite unfit for this great command at this time of crisis in our Nation's history. But I thought it sufficient to tell the King that I had "doubts" about the selection.[4]

Though some historians contend that Haig schemed from the beginning to supplant French as commander in chief of the BEF, such was not the case. In a diary entry two days later Haig outlined his intention to "behave as I did in the South African War, namely to be thoroughly loyal and do my duty as a subordinate should, trying all the time to see Sir John's good qualities and not his weak ones."[5] Though an open break was something beyond Haig's moral code and Haig remained loyal to French for the time being, he also retained close ties to the King and to Kitchener—ties he would later use as the continued strain of war brought the command structure of the BEF to the breaking point.

As the BEF made its way to the continent, with Haig's arrival taking place on August 16, the vast French and German military machines moved forward with their respective war plans. General Joseph Joffre, the French commander in chief, prosecuted an invasion of Alsace-Lorraine, but his First and Second Armies faced unexpectedly stiff resistance and gained little ground. Indeed, the Germans, under the command of General Hemluth von Moltke, had altered the Schlieffen Plan to account for a stronger defense against the French attack. Further north, a weakened but still formidable German force of some sixty divisions launched their great attempt at envelopment and first steamrolled through Belgium. Fatefully, the British forces, form-ing up near Maubeuge for an advance to Mons, would stand squarely in the path of the mighty German advance.

As French efforts to advance in the south failed, intelligence began to trickle in regarding the massive nature of the German offensive in the north. Haig heard the rumors and wondered if the tiny BEF was advancing to its doom. He was quite correct to be concerned, for on August 23 the German First Army, under the command of General Alexander von Kluck, slammed into the BEF outside Mons. Severely outnumbered, the BEF fought well, holding off the German advance and avoiding disaster. The battle was, in the main, prosecuted by II Corps under the com-mand of General Horace Smith-Dorrien, who had been given the command by Kitchener over French's objections, further straining their fragile relationship.

With both flanks exposed following a French withdrawal, the BEF extricated itself from battle and began a harrowing retreat of its own, lasting for thirteen days and traversing nearly two hundred miles under great strain and pressure from the un-remitting German advance. The situation was so muddled dur-ing the retreat from Mons that Haig once nearly drove into the German lines, and on the night of the twenty-fifth was unchar-acteristically unnerved by a German advance into the British bil-let area at Landrecies. Even so, Haig remained in firm control, and the BEF succeeded in executing one of the most difficult of all military maneuvers—a retreat under fire.

Though it was once again II Corps that faced the brunt of the German offensive, fighting a second sharp engagement at Le Cateau, the retreat placed an almost unbearable strain on the en-tire BEF. The situation was so bad that on August 30, French proposed to take the BEF out of the line to refit. Only pressure from both Kitchener and Joffre forced French to relent and served to sustain his flagging morale.[6] Though Haig's spirit char-acteristically remained rather more resilient, the epic retreat also had an important effect on his thinking. Neither French nor Haig had ever entirely trusted the abilities or the intentions of their French allies. As French actions consistently left his flank exposed and disrupted his own logistic plans for retreat, Haig's annoyance grew ever greater. He even described the French as, "so unreliable. One cannot believe a word they say as a rule."[7] Haig realized that the French in many ways controlled the Allied war effort, and he would make every effort to conform to their designs. However, he first and foremost remained loyal to Britain and the BEF. The subtle interplay between the forces competing for Haig's loyalty, the need to cooperate with the French, and his overarching dedication to the BEF remained a central theme for the remainder of the conflict. On many occasions Haig would subsume his own planning for the greater good of the Alliance, but he always retained a healthy suspicion of French motives and abilities.

While the BEF was in retreat the realities of the Great War would begin to assert themselves in earnest. Finally realizing that his beloved Plan 17 had come to ruin, Joffre only belatedly reacted to the massive German advance in the north. Though the situation was critical, Joffre exhibited a surety of purpose and a confidence that would also come to epitomize the personality of Douglas Haig. Unperturbed by impending disaster, Joffre shifted his forces northward in an effort to halt the German advance before it reached Paris. It was a gargantuan and complicated task, but Joffre was able to rely on lateral rail communications to make good his move, while the Germans could only advance at the speed of marching soldiers. In what would become one of the driving strategic realities of the Great War, Joffre's shift northward demonstrated that defenders could always react, moving troops laterally more quickly than attackers could advance. Even before the onset of trench warfare the great German advance of 1914 fell victim to the realities of the time, for the advantage in World War I would forever lie with the defender.

By September 5, the German offensive had lost much of its momentum, in part because of logistical difficulties and poor leadership. As a result the German armies were forced to wheel to the east of Paris, offering their vulnerable flank to the gathering Allied forces. Joffre seized his chance and ordered an attack, having to press a now quite reluctant Field Marshal French to commit the BEF to the scheme. The resultant Battle of the Marne, in which the BEF played an important role, was a close-run and rather confused affair that ended when Moltke in effect lost command of his forces, leading to a German retreat from the gates of Paris to defensive positions on the Aisne River. During the struggle French's optimism returned and he dared hope again for a quick and decisive victory over the retreating Germans. Haig was also momentarily swept up in the enthusiasm, even questioning his own belief in a long war.[8] However, as I Corps gained contact with the German defenses along the Aisne, Haig quickly realized that the nature of the war had changed. In a brief struggle Haig's force failed to dent the rather sketchy German defensive network. To Haig, a devotee of mobile warfare, the static, positional battle along the Aisne was confusing in nature. He was not alone, for the resulting fighting was anathema to both the Germans and the Allies, who desperately attempted to maintain a war of movement by a series of outflanking movements toward the north—but a war of attrition had already begun.[9]

In the period rather inappropriately known as the "race to the sea," both French and German forces moved north at relatively the same speed in vain attempts to locate an open flank. Soon combatant forces reached the English Channel, with control of the Belgian ports of Ostende and Zeebrugge falling to the Germans. Though unexpected at the time, German control over the ports and the resultant threat to British shipping and control of the Channel would become central to British wartime thinking and strategy. French, who had regained his confidence and was quite attracted to the idea of operations along the coast in cooperation with the Royal Navy, fully supported the Allied northward movement. Joffre, however, remained skeptical of British intentions, believing that location near the coast would only make a BEF retreat to Britain more likely if disaster once again ensued.[10]

As events to the north ran their course Haig's I Corps disengaged from battle on the Aisne and made its way into the Allied line near the Belgian city of Ypres. Fired by optimism and believing that the German forces to its front were weak and disorganized, French ordered the BEF to advance from Ypres to capture Bruges. French indeed hoped that the BEF would now play its great role in the decisive battle that would turn the tide of war. Though Haig greeted the orders with optimism, information from his controversial intelligence chief, Brigadier General John Charteris, indicated that the Germans were present near Ypres in much greater numbers than French had anticipated.[11] In fact General Erich von Falkenhayen, who had supplanted Moltke as commander in chief, had shifted a great weight of German forces to the area in an effort to break through the Allied lines and drive to the coast, hoping to make the BEF quit the war. Thus as British forces moved to the offensive, they ran headlong into the advancing German armies, with the Germans enjoying a local superiority in troop strength of five to one.

On October 19, the twin attacks crashed together outside Ypres. Haig soon realized that the Germans were greatly superior in numbers, and were not retreating as expected, but were instead launching a very dangerous attack. French, though, remained confused regarding the reality of the situation for several days—committing additional forces to a fruitless offensive when he should have been concentrating on desperate defensive measures. After a series of disorganized encounter battles Falkenhayen seized the initiative on October 31, by launching a major effort to shatter the British lines near Gheluvelt along the famed Menin Road. The bulk of the offensive broke against Haig's I Corps, and the resulting situation quickly developed into one of the most important moments of the entire war. The strength of the German assault forced the British cavalry off of the strategic Messines Ridge, cavalry forces that had been operating effectively as mounted infantry. However, the most critical moment of the battle came near Gheluvelt.

With fairly little subtlety the massed German force rushed the lines of the British First Division. Concentrated defensive fire caused the Germans fearsome losses, but still Gheluvelt fell and the lines of the First Division very nearly shattered. As the fluid situation ebbed and flowed, Haig enjoyed only intermittent contact with his frontline troops. Dissatisfied amid the confusion and realizing that the situation was dire Haig decided to ride to the front in an effort to gather information and to rally his forces. Unbeknownst to him, at the same time a counterattack by the Second Worcesters had reclaimed the situation and convinced Falkenhayen that victory was beyond his grasp that day. Thus Haig's decision to move forward was not critical to the battle, but serves to testify to his personal bravery. The battle had been a very close-run thing, and in reality the BEF had come very close to disaster, averted when Falkenhayen misinterpreted the situation and failed to press home his advantage. Some historians claim that the near German victory was formative to Haig's World War I experience. Had Falkenhayn only persevered he might have achieved success. As a result, in similar situations Haig would choose to persevere long after the hope of victory had passed.[12]

After a comparative lull in the fighting, during which the rates of attrition and exertion remained high, on November 11 the Germans launched their final major attempt to break the Allied positions. Though much of the fighting again fell to Haig's depleted I Corps, French forces continued to play a major role in the battle and indeed the decisive role in the overall struggle. Haig, however, remained concerned regarding French planning and fighting ability, contending that their commanders still exhibited a propensity to retreat, leaving British forces vulnerable. He evidenced his frustrations in a diary entry stating that the French should, "treat us fairly! Because ever since we landed in France they seem ready to drain the last drop of blood out of the British force!"[13]

The weight of the German attack concentrated again in the area around the Menin Road. Though the Germans nearly achieved a decisive success, the BEF held firm, finally repulsing the German advance with heavy losses. Though the fighting lingered, in tandem with the French the BEF had won a victory in the First Battle of Ypres, but at a high cost. In fact the BEF that had crossed to France at the beginning of the war had ceased to exist. The First Battle of Ypres alone had cost Britain 50,000 casualties. Haig's I Corps, with a normal establishment of 18,000 men, had been reduced to 68 officers and 2,776 other ranks. The BEF was a spent force, and would be replaced in the line by the burgeoning numbers of the Kitchener Army and other units called in from around the globe. In the wake of First Ypres, Haig's I Corps left the line to refit, and Haig, now promoted to full general, went on a short leave in Britain. In France and Flanders both opposing forces began to dig in for the winter. The war of movement, the conflict that Haig knew so well and was prepared to fight, had come to a conclusion. The hell of trench warfare was about to begin.

Chapter 3

Commander of the BEF

As both combatant forces began to dig in during the winter of 1914–1915 the nature of World War I changed fundamentally. Instead of the mobile and decisive warfare that Haig had been taught to expect at Staff College and had prepared for ever since, the Great War settled down into a trench stalemate that seemingly defied solution. Though the trench systems of 1915 were rudimentary, they would soon be transformed into defensive networks miles in depth, protected by massive belts of barbed wire, studded with daunting strong points, and bristling with defensive firepower. The vexing problem seemed rather simple in nature. What was the best way to evict defending forces from their trench networks, thus reinstating a war of movement and making decisive victory possible?

Trench warfare in actuality proved to be a riddle with a very difficult solution, for everything in the Great War favored the defender. Once dug in, defending forces could use the defensive prowess of newly developed machine guns and quick-firing artillery pieces to call down a "storm of steel," capable of obliterating an army caught in the open waste of no-man's-land. These same weapons systems that so dominated the Great War, though, were of little use to attackers. Machine guns were initially far too heavy and cumbersome for offensive purposes. Artillery, though quite deadly, was being used for the first time in an exclusive "indirect fire" mode. In essence the gunners were firing at targets they could not see—sometimes up to fifteen miles distant. Though the artillery would make quantum leaps in ability during the Great War, it was at first hopelessly inaccurate, making the destruction of enemy trenches and strong points virtually impossible. In fact artillery was so inaccurate that if a gun fired one hundred shells at an unseen trench, only two would register direct hits, and, taking production problems into consideration, chances were that one of the direct hits would be a dud.[1] Infantry, with their bayonets and rifles, were of little use against an entrenched foe, unable either to cut through barbed wire unaided or to seize enemy strong points alone. Thus the state of weaponry during the Great War tilted the delicate balance of warfare toward the defender.

Finally, attacking forces in the Great War lacked two all-important things: communications and a weapon of exploitation. Before World War I commanders had been able to see their battlefield and control it through the use of runners. Robert E. Lee, for instance, could often see almost the entire battlefield and was able to issue instructions to his forces with relative ease. The Industrial Revolution, however, changed that. Battlefields were now vast, often covering hundreds of miles. Communications technology, though, had not kept pace. World War II commanders could rely on radio communications to control their forces, but commanders in the Great War did not have that luxury, for their radios were primitive and cumbersome. In World War I once attacking forces left their trenches, commanders virtually lost all contact with their men, and thus all control of the battle.[2]

Civil War and Napoleonic generals had a weapon upon which to rely that afforded the chance to convert victory into a rout: Haig's beloved cavalry. On the western front, though, cavalry would prove to be of limited use, even more vulnerable than infantry when caught in the open. After World War I generals could rely on the speed of armor to win lightning-quick victories over defending forces. Thus the Great War was the single modern war that lacked a weapon of exploitation, that could use speed to transform a tactical victory into a strategic advance—the very goal taught so well in staff colleges across Europe.

On the offensive, then, Great War generals were at a tremendous disadvantage in weaponry. Battles could not effectively be commanded because of lack of communications, and armies could only advance as fast as their feet allowed. Defenders, though, suffered fewer communication woes. Able to make use of telegraph and telephone communications and rail transport far behind the lines, defenders always knew more about the battle than attackers and could rush reinforcements to the scene to stem any possible breakthrough. The technological realities of the turn of the century thus dictated a defensive war. Defenders could outshoot, out-think, and outmaneuver attackers.[3]

Haig and the other commanders of the Great War were, in many ways, nineteenth century military leaders thrust into the first industrial, total war of the twentieth century. Militarily raised on the primacy of the offensive and the central importance of morale, Haig now found himself in a war dominated by firepower and the defensive. Thus Haig faced one of the most daunting problems provided by modern military history. Lacking the proper weaponry and communications, how should the BEF, in tandem with the French, endeavor to overcome the defensive prowess of the German trench system in an effort to achieve victory? The current nature of weaponry and communications stood against the notion of attack. Indeed many historians claim that Haig's own training and temperament also mitigated against the innovation needed to find a solution to trench warfare.[4] Seemingly against all odds, though, during the coming years of the Great War, eventually the BEF would adapt to the realities of trench warfare, making use of difficult on-the-job military training, increasing military professionalism, and advances in technology to solve the riddle of trench warfare and thus lay the foundations of truly modern war. Historians, though, remain divided as to whether Douglas Haig played an indispensable role in the improvement of the British military or whether he was a deterrent to change and thus caused the needless loss of thousands of lives.

At the close of 1914 French had reorganized the BEF into two armies, with Haig in command of First Army, which comprised I Corps, IV Corps, and the Indian Corps. While the French mustered rather sporadic assaults against the German salient in central France during the winter, the BEF was refitting and pondering its strategic options. French and Haig were certain of one thing: that the war, though difficult, would only be won in the western front, and that any diversion of resources to other theaters of war was misguided. In early 1915 French supported the idea of a British attack along the Belgian coast aimed at turning the Germans out of Ostende and Zeebrugge, an idea that would also strike Haig's fancy and remain part of his strategic thinking for the remainder of the conflict. Joffre predictably argued against such a course of action, instead supporting a combined Franco-British offensive designed to drive the Germans from France.

French, though he had some support from Kitchener, also met considerable resistance for his planning within the British government. Beginning what is known as the "Easterner-Westerner Debate," several British politicians, notably David Lloyd George, favored using the strength of the British fleet to strike at less stalwart foes than Germany. The debate would rage throughout the Great War, with varying results, and with Haig a constant advocate of the necessity of defeating the Germans on the western front. In this instance, though, French lost the argument, resulting in men and matériel being diverted from the western front for offensive action first in the Dardanelles and later at Gallipoli aimed against the Ottoman Empire.[5] French now found his forces stretched thin and as a result had to abandon independent offensive action in favor of closer cooperation with the French military. The rather haphazard method of Allied strategic and tactical planning would remain a glaring deficiency until the onset of a truly unified system of coalition warfare in 1918.

Joffre's plan for combined action called first for a Franco-British assault on the Aubers Ridge, which would serve as a diversion before the main French assault in Champagne. French agreed to the idea and placed the planning for the battle in the hands of Haig, who chose to attack in the area around Neuve Chapelle. A complication quickly developed when Joffre announced the cancellation of the French portion of the fighting at Neuve Chapelle, but French decided to go ahead with the planned offensive on his own. The resulting Battle of Neuve Chapelle was the first major British offensive of the Great War and was formative to Haig's military development. It was to be his first true test of command, and it set precedents and trends he would follow for the remainder of the conflict.

In early February 1915, Haig turned planning of the proposed offensive at Neuve Chapelle over to General Sir Henry Rawlinson, Commander of IV Corps. The fact that Haig hoped that planning for the offensive would take only ten days serves as another indicator that he, like the other commanders of his time, still had much to learn about the realities of combat in the Great War. Rawlinson also demonstrated that he too had much to learn by dawdling over his planning and then finally producing a rather complicated and unworkable scheme for a dual assault on Neuve Chapelle. Haig overruled his subordinate and suggested an assault carried out in a more "simple common sense way."[6] Rawlinson adjusted his planning accordingly, and chose to rely upon a massive artillery barrage to subdue the rather rudimentary German defenses around Neuve Chapelle. Since infantry could have but little effect on entrenched defenders, artillery was obviously the way forward in the Great War. Though opinions varied, Rawlinson and Haig decided to rely at this juncture on a bombardment of short duration in an effort to retain the element of surprise. To their credit Rawlinson and

Haig managed to gather 340 artillery pieces, the weaponry of four divisions plus heavier guns drawn from Britain, for the offensive. The number, though dwarfed by artillery amassed later in the conflict, represented one gun for every six yards of enemy trench in the area of the assault. Though the weight of shell was prodigious, the artillery, unable accurately to strike what it could not see, faced a stern test. In essence the fortunes of the entire battle rested with the artillery, which had to crush the German wire, destroy German strong points, hinder German reinforcement, and silence the defending German artillery. The task was simply too vast.

Rawlinson planned for his infantry to advance in column formations in the wake of the crushing artillery barrage and to seize the wreckage of Neuve Chapelle. Haig, however, wanted more and again altered Rawlinson's plan, instructing that:

> The advance to be made is not a minor operation. It must be understood that we are embarking on a serious offensive movement with the object of breaking the German line and consequently our advance is to be pushed vigorously. Very likely an operation of considerable magnitude may result.
>
> The idea is not to capture a trench here, or a trench there, but to carry the operation right through; in a sense surprise the Germans, carry them right off their legs, push forward to the Aubers . . . ridge with as little delay as possible and exploit the success thus gained by pushing forward mounted troops forthwith.[7]

Given his training and belief system, at this point in the war it is to be expected that Haig hoped for great things, even from a rather limited offensive. After hearing his chief's scheme, Rawlinson, whether out of duty or out of conviction, quickly became a convert to the desire to aim for greater goals. Though Haig was not alone in his desires or his belief in the possibility of a breakthrough offensive it was at this point that one of the fundamental arguments of the Great War was born. Should offensives aim for distant objectives or more limited goals? In hindsight it is easy to realize that overly ambitious offensives in World War I would come to grief. However, neither Haig nor

Rawlinson could have realized the changed nature of war in the buildup to Neuve Chapelle. The most important question, though, is what would these men and others like them across the western front learn from their mistakes?

Haig's offensive at Neuve Chapelle finally rolled forward on March 10, following a thirty-five-minute bombardment. The British Seventh and Eighth Divisions, along with the Indian Corps—numbering some twelve thousand men—attacked, facing only two thousand German defenders in a forward trench backed by concrete machine gun strong points. Though Rawlinson's forces held the initial advantage, he realized that it would not hold long, for he estimated that the Germans could rush sixteen thousand reinforcements to the battle area within two days—necessitating Haig's desire for a quick advance. Initially the attack went quite well, the stunned Germans offering little resistance as Neuve Chapelle itself fell by mid-morning. However, in the center of the line the Twenty-third Brigade and the Indian Corps to the south had rather slower going in part because of poor artillery preparation. Thus the opening phase of the offensive was rather a mixed bag.

Due to poor communications, though, Rawlinson knew little of what transpired, and Haig even less. Reliant upon runners, the news that Rawlinson received regarding his advancing forces was often incorrect and always out of date. In the most famous example, when Rawlinson finally received notice of the stranded Twenty-third Brigade he altered his planning to aid in its advance. By the time his orders were carried out, though, a renewed bombardment had enabled the Twenty-third to gain its objectives. At the same time further south elements of the Twenty-fifth Brigade had driven through the main German defenses and halted while awaiting reinforcements and orders. Because he learned too late that success beckoned in the south, the opportunity for a possible breakthrough in the area had passed before Rawlinson could react. Thus because of the communications problems Rawlinson had, he would continue to misuse his reserve forces during Neuve Chapelle. That the Twenty-fifth

Brigade had seemingly very nearly achieved a breakthrough would be critical to Haig's conclusions regarding the battle. It seemed that the formula for success had worked, but the system had failed. In actuality, though, a breakthrough had never really beckoned, for the Germans had already rushed reinforcements to the scene and stood ready to face a renewed assault.[8]

On the afternoon of March 10 Rawlinson finally gathered his reinforcements together to leapfrog through his advanced lines toward Aubers Ridge, but the resulting attack was a confused failure. Having no time to register their weapons on the new German defenses, the covering artillery bombardment was short and ineffective, even raining down on the newly won British lines. On the following day the British struck again, but now faced considerable German reinforcements in a maze of newly constructed and unobserved defensive positions. The covering artillery bombardment lasted only fifteen minutes and was hopelessly inaccurate. The artillery had had a great deal of time to prepare for the first day's assault, locating German trenches and strong points and preregistering fire. On the second day, though, many of the artillery pieces had been moved and there had been no preregistration. In fact it was not known where many of the new German defenses were located. Thus the artillery fired blind, and failed to destroy the German wire or to silence the growing German defensive fire. Predictably the attack came to grief, with many men being shot down as soon as they exited their own trenches. On the third day of the battle the Germans mounted a stiff counterattack, only to be mown down in their turn, with a subsequent British attack again gaining but little. Realizing that the initiative had been lost, Haig and Rawlinson brought the Battle of Neuve Chapelle to a close after only three days. The British had penetrated the German lines to a depth of 1,000 meters and captured Neuve Chapelle at a cost of twelve thousand casualties while inflicting a similar number of losses on the Germans.

In retrospect the results of Neuve Chapelle point out many of the weaknesses of the offensive in the Great War. Having

The Western Front, 1915

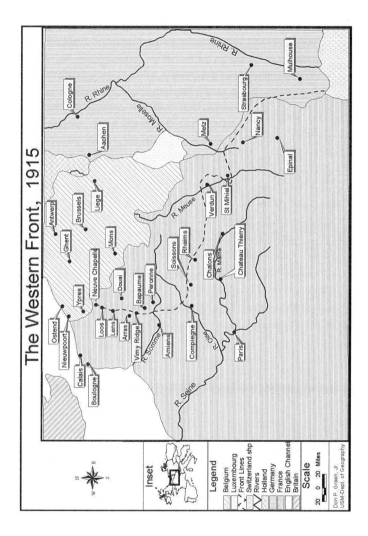

Inset

Legend

Belgium
Luxembourg
Front Lines
Switzerland.shp
Rivers
Germany
Holland
France
English Channel
Britain

Scale

20 0 20 Miles

Don P. Green, Jr.
USM-Dept. of Geography

Mulhouse

R. Rhine

Strasbourg

Cologne

R. Rhine

R. Moselle

Metz

Nancy

Aachen

Epinal

Antwerp

Brussels

Liege

R. Meuse

Verdun

St Mihiel

Ghent

Mons

Neuve Chapelle

Soissons

Rheims

Chalons

R. Marne

Chateau Thierry

Ypres

Douai

Bapaume

Peronne

Ostend

Loos

Lens

Arras

Nieuwpoort

Vimy Ridge

R. Somme

Amiens

Compiegne

R. Oise

Paris

Calais

Boulogne

R. Seine

achieved surprise and under the cover of a meticulous bombardment, British forces were able to advance with relative ease against the first line of German defenses. Very quickly, though, the realities of the Great War had conspired to dash British hopes. Rawlinson had been unable effectively to command the battle because of poor communications. The Germans had been able to react with great speed to the threat, tipping the balance against the British. Thus the attack had very quickly lost its momentum, even while the main weapon of the attacker, artillery, had become less and less effective due to the fluidity of the battlefield situation. The realities of the Great War would place a definite life span on offensive actions, allowing attackers to break in to the enemy defensive systems, but never to break through. Again, though, these lessons are part of historical hindsight, a blessing not granted to Haig and Rawlinson, who were left to learn their own lessons from the battle.

As it happens, Rawlinson and Haig drew quite different conclusions from Neuve Chapelle. For his part Rawlinson focused on the power of well-sited artillery to allow the infantry access to the German frontline trenches. As a result Rawlinson became one of the first and most important proponents of "bite and hold" tactics.

> What we want to do now is what I call 'bite and hold'. Bite off a piece of the enemy's line, like Neuve Chapelle, and hold it against counter attack. The bite can be made without much loss, and, if we choose the right place & make every preparation to put it quickly in a state of defence there ought to be no difficulty in holding it against the enemy's counter attacks & inflicting on him at least twice the loss we have suffered in making the bite.[9]

The drawback to Rawlinson's plan, of course, was that it would require a vast number of such bites to make a significant dent in the German lines, resulting in an unthinkable war of attrition.

Haig, though, remained more optimistic, focusing on the seeming missed opportunity afforded on the first day of the offensive. Believing that if the command malfunctions of the day could be mastered breakthrough was still possible, Haig looked to make good the mistakes of Neuve Chapelle and still believed in decisive battle.[10] Haig was certainly not alone in his thinking, for most of the leading commanders of the Great War, from Joffre to Ludendorff, retained a similar adherence to the idea of breakthrough and a restoration of a war of movement. Thus, though some important lessons had been learned from Neuve Chapelle, the "learning curve" had only just begun.

Spurred onward by their recent success, though they had differing interpretations of its meaning, French, Haig, and Rawlinson all favored a renewal of the British offensive on Aubers Ridge, again as part of a plan to divert forces from a proposed French offensive further south. Falkenhayen, though, preempted Allied planning by launching a second German offensive in Flanders. The Second Battle of Ypres, marked by the first major use of poison gas in the Great War, involved mainly the Second Army under the command of Smith-Dorrien, leaving Haig to work on his proposed offensive, but the continued diversion of military resources to the war against the Ottoman Empire and a growing and controversial shortage of artillery shells played havoc with Haig's planning. He had hoped to renew the offensive with greater strength than before, hoping also to achieve greater goals. However, by May Haig realized that his strength was too limited to achieve a great result, and he adjusted his planning accordingly, aiming at more limited objectives.[11]

When the IV Corps moved forward into the Battle of Aubers Ridge on May 9, though, the results were even less than Haig had expected. Though the weight of the artillery barrage at Aubers Ridge was similar to that of Neuve Chapelle, it had to cover a much more dense German defensive system, thus diluting its effectiveness. In essence, then, the all-important bombardment at Aubers Ridge was only one-fifth the intensity of that at Neuve Chapelle.[12] Faced with much stronger German defensive works, including a triple line of trenches, and covered by a much weaker and inaccurate barrage, the assault at Aubers

Ridge gained very little ground. Though initially hoping to reverse the failure, Haig—much to his credit—called off the offensive immediately.

The failure of the barrage, owing in part to technical reasons such as wear on artillery barrels and weather conditions, gave Haig pause. It seemed that there remained several problems inherent in the attack that had yet to be solved before decisive battle could be waged. As a result, though the French, who were attacking further south at Vimy Ridge, asked for an immediate continuation of the British offensive, Haig pressed French for permission to wait. Haig informed his chief that:

> The defences on our front are so carefully and so strongly made, and mutual support with machine-guns so complete, that in order to demolish them a long methodical bombardment will be necessary by heavy artillery (guns and howitzers) before Infantry are sent forward to attack. . . . Accurate observations of each shot will be arranged so as to make sure of flattening out the enemy's 'strong points' of support, before the Infantry is launched.[13]

Haig instead favored a much more methodical assault aimed at overwhelming the system of German strong points.[14] Thus, though Haig still contended that a breakthrough was possible, he believed that it could only be achieved through a preponderance of artillery fire and a great weight of infantry. When those conditions did not exist he was quite satisfied with and able to prosecute battles that were more limited in nature, adhering to Rawlinson's "bite and hold" technique.

Six days later the First Army again attacked, beginning the Battle of Festubert. The ten-day offensive was successful in many areas, penetrating the German lines to a depth of 1,000 meters at a cost of sixteen thousand casualties. Though predictably the greatest gains of the offensive came in its earliest moments, the overall results were much more like those of Neuve Chapelle and helped to restore the confidence of both Haig and French in decisive victory. A following minor offensive at Givenchy in June did nothing to alter Haig's enthusiasm. Following the battle a period of relative inactivity set in for nearly three months as French began to plan for the next major British offensive. However, during the lull in the fighting a storm broke upon the political scene that would lead to Haig taking command of the BEF.

French, who was under great pressure to achieve dramatic results on the western front, blamed much of his continued failure on a growing and critical lack of artillery shells. The leadership of the BEF had reached the conclusion that weight of artillery fire was of paramount importance to a successful advance, and French blamed Kitchener for the shortage that was so debilitating to his success. Fearing for his command, French leaked the story of the shell shortage, telling war correspondent Charles Repington that it was "a fatal bar to our success."[15] The resultant "shell scandal" caused great controversy and helped to hasten the fall of the Asquith regime and the formation of a coalition wartime government. Kitchener, though his prestige was weakened, remained in office, and his already strained relations with and confidence in French suffered greatly. Though Haig avoided direct involvement in the controversy his connections to both Kitchener and to the King remained close and intact. At the same time Haig grew ever more certain that the mercurial, and now more vulnerable, French was not the proper man to command the BEF.

Joffre remained convinced of the usefulness of one further great combined offensive in the west before the close of the year. Though Haig advocated yet another operation in the area of Aubers Ridge, Joffre pressed for an assault at the conjunction of the French and British armies near the town of Loos. After surveying the area Haig commented that the ground to be covered was quite difficult, including many coal slag heaps. For this reason he and French both initially advocated a more limited assault—in Haig's words, "to be made chiefly with artillery and I am not to launch a large force of infantry to the attack of objectives which are so strongly held as to result only in the sacrifice of many lives." Joffre, aided by Kitchener, instead pushed for a greater British commitment, and French "decided that we must act with all our energy, and do our utmost to help the French, even though, by so doing, we suffered very heavy losses indeed." [16] Thus Haig and Rawlinson came to plan the Battle of Loos. Both men, vacillating between the options of bite and hold and the attempt at a breakthrough, made ready for an offensive designed to overthrow the powerful German defenses in the area and advance to depth.

With relatively little interference from Haig, Rawlinson drew up the tactical plan of advance. Once again reliant on artillery support and preparation, IV Corps, which now contained many untried Kitchener Army units, made ready to assault Loos and Hill 70 before breaking into and through the second line of German defenses in the area. Despite careful planning, though, the artillery preparation was less than perfect. Using 251 artillery pieces, IV Corps enjoyed artillery cover of only one-fifth as strong as that at Neuve Chapelle. Again the difficulties were caused by shell shortages and stronger and more numerous German defensive positions. In some areas where the artillery fire was adequate, great gains would accrue. However, in others the wire would not even be cut, leading to disaster. [17]

For his part Haig spent much of his time leading up to the battle dealing with the question of reserves. Haig had learned with the supposed missed opportunity at Neuve Chapelle that adequate reserves had to be on hand very close to the front lines, ready to make use of any fleeting opportunity to seize the initiative. The scope of the coming offensive, however, left IV Corps without an organic reserve force. Thus the main reserves for the battle—the Twenty-first, Twenty-fourth, and the Guards Divisions—remained under the control of French himself. Haig pressed for the ability to place the reserves as close to the line as deemed possible. However, French demurred and Haig began the Battle of Loos with his reserve formations, in his mind, too far back from the front to make a critical difference in the battle. [18]

On September 25, after a four-day artillery barrage and the first major British use of poison gas, Rawlinson's leading divisions launched their assault. On the right flank the Forty-seventh Division achieved its initial goals and served as a flank guard. Further to the left, the First Division met with serious resistance and faced a great deal of uncut barbed wire; it advanced only rather slowly. Again communication difficulties served to muddle the situation, costing Rawlinson valuable time in sorting out the difficulties on the left flank. In the center, though, a great opportunity seemed to beckon. The Fifteenth Division, though it suffered heavy initial losses, broke through the German frontline trench and quickly seized the tactically important Hill 70. At this point Haig hoped to throw the reserves into the battle, but they were located too far behind the line to do any good. The opportunity to break through the German lines had vanished, in Haig's mind, as a result of French's continued mismanagement.[19]

As at Neuve Chapelle, though, there remains considerable doubt as to whether any opportunity beckoned at all. The exhausted men on Hill 70 now faced an intact German second line trench, with very little in the way of artillery support. In addition the Germans were predictably rushing reinforcements to the scene. Again, in historical hindsight it is clear that the timely arrival of the reserves would not have achieved a great victory. However, to Haig the circumstantial evidence of Loos indicated that, like Neuve Chapelle, a breakthrough had beckoned.

Chagrined that the opportunity had been lost, but undaunted, Haig committed the reserve forces to battle on the second day of the offensive. With minimal artillery support the Twenty-first and Twenty-fourth Divisions assaulted the intact and recently reinforced German lines to the east of Hill 70 with disastrous results. Though the tempo of the battle then slowed considerably, the French, still attacking further south, required a continuation of the British offensive to draw off German reserves. Thus the Battle of Loos lingered on until October 16, eventually achieving meager additional gains at the cost of over fifty thousand casualties.

The failure to achieve victory at Loos had capped a poor year for the BEF. Despite a heavy loss of life, victory had not been forthcoming and elements of the government and the popular press clamored for a change of Britain's wartime leadership. In London Kitchener received much of the blame, while French was the obvious villain of the piece on the battlefront. Haig and other leading officers had also come to the conclusion that French was now too great a liability to the war effort. For Haig much of his growing discontent with French centered around the controversial role of the reserve forces at Loos. French and Kitchener were both ready for a fall, and Haig had just disagreements with both men. While he did undoubtedly play a role in their demise, it seems fairly certain that Haig did not play that role in an attempt to gain higher position. Haig was rightly concerned that the highest level of leadership of the British military had failed in its assigned duties.

In the coming political turmoil Haig corresponded in the main with both Kitchener himself and with the King. Haig also corresponded with General Sir William Robertson, then serving as French's chief of staff, who was in London at the behest of the government and who was himself on the brink of a career breakthrough. In October Haig made his position abundantly clear to King George V, who bluntly asked Haig his opinion of French:

> I told him that I thought the time to have removed French was after the Retreat, because he had so mismanaged matters, and shown in the handling of the small Expeditionary Force in the Field a great ignorance of the essential principles of war. Since then, during the trench warfare, the Army had grown larger and I thought at first there was no great scope for French to go wrong. I have therefore done my utmost to stop criticisms and make matters run smoothly. But French's handling of the reserves in the last battle, his obstinacy, and conceit, showed his incapacity, and it seemed to me impossible for anyone to prevent him doing the same things again. I therefore thought strongly, that, for the sake of the Empire, French ought to be removed.[20]

Though Haig's actions were not central to the issue, the military regime and uneasy alliance between Kitchener and French came crashing down in December 1915. Kitchener remained in office as Secretary of State for War, but had his executive powers greatly reduced. Instead Robertson took over as chief of a revitalized Imperial General Staff and would serve in that capacity as the principal military advisor to the government. French was relegated to leading the Home Forces in Britain, and Haig took French's place as commander in chief of the burgeoning British Expeditionary Force.

Thus Haig, partly through ability and partly through political connections, had risen to the most important military command in British history. As the principal architect of many of the major battles of the BEF in 1915 Haig undoubtedly had the most applicable experience of any possible candidate for the job. In his new position Haig would draw upon the lessons that he had learned in the difficult battles of 1915 to point him toward victory in subsequent, much larger, offensives under his command. Though he had learned that attrition and methodical advance had their place in battle, something much more substantial seemed possible if only the BEF could overcome problems of communication, use of reserves, and artillery performance. In the words of historian Paddy Griffith:

> One point that is often missed about these small and unsuccessful battles of 1915 is that several of them could show at least a few moments when the infantry actually came very close to complete victory. At both Neuve Chapelle and Loos some of the assaulting divisions experienced the heady sensation of walking calmly across No Man's Land in their regulation waves, without undue interference from the enemy. . . . Admittedly such successes had a lot to do with the state of the German defences, the cleverness of BEF staffwork and the intensity of the artillery preparation; but to many infantry commanders it must have seemed as though there had been no real break from the nineteenth-century experience. In the past it had generally been possible for massed column attacks to roll over even the most formidable defences, given the right sort of preparation: and now in 1915 exactly the same phenomenon seemed to be repeated.[21]

Chapter 4

The Death of a Generation?
The Battle of the Somme

T HE TASK facing Haig upon his assumption of the command of the BEF was daunting in a strategic sense, but also in a purely practical sense. Britain's army had historically always been rather small, but during the Great War, because of an influx of volunteers, the BEF mushroomed in size, becoming the largest army Britain had ever, or would ever, put into the field. At the beginning of the conflict the BEF numbered 120,000 men, but by December 1915 the tiny force had risen to a strength of 986,000, to 1.5 million by July 1916, and above 1.8 million throughout the remainder of the war. Haig and his staff did well in dealing with the gargantuan and unforeseen task of supply and control of such a large military force. The administration of "discipline, promotion, leave, movements of units, bath-houses, mail, supplies of boots, whale-oil, plum and apple jam, barbed wire, planks for roads and trenches, forage and fodder, placed an administrative burden on the staff beyond anything imagined before 1914." Though certainly not all of the day-to-day managerial drudgery of the BEF fell to Haig, he was "thus principal director of Britain's newest and greatest corporate enterprise, comparable in size to the administration of the largest city in the Kingdom (with the sole exception of London), the governance of which was the more delicate since it was based within a jealous and suspicious foreign state."[1] Though the BEF certainly made mistakes in its logistical prosecution of the Great War, levels of supply remained consistently high and the military machine in general ran smoothly. Under the crushing burden of the war the morale of the British soldiery also remained stable, in large part because of close officer-man relations but also to the care taken by high command.[2] Thus, that the BEF alone of the armies that entered the war in 1914 did not suffer from a major mutiny is in part a testament to a forgotten, often behind-the-scenes, aspect of the leadership of Douglas Haig.

The over-quick expansion of the BEF also posed other significant problems of command, for the rank and file of the Kitchener armies pouring into France had until only recently been civilians. Their training had been rather rudimentary, as Haig had earlier feared, leaving many to wonder whether or not the new soldiers would be able to stand the stress of battle or prosecute complex infantry maneuvers. That Haig realized the deficiencies in the training of his men is obvious. In March 1916 Kitchener warned Haig to husband the strength of the BEF. Haig responded:

> I said that I had never had any intention of attacking with all available troops except in an emergency to save the French from disaster, and Paris perhaps from capture. Meantime, I am strengthening the long line which I have recently taken over, and training the troops. I have not got an Army in France really, but a collection of divisions untrained for the Field. The actual fighting Army will be evolved from them.[3]

In addition the rapid expansion of the BEF meant that inexperienced commanders now found themselves leading much larger formations. The men who now commanded the five armies that made up the BEF had been at best only divisional commanders in 1914. Most of the corps commanders had then only led brigades, and divisional commanders had started the war commanding battalions.[4] In essence, then, the leadership of the BEF, with the exceptions of Haig and Rawlinson, had never before led a unit larger than a division into battle. From the highest to the lowest level the BEF was an untried, amateur force that required "on the job" training. It was but the beginning of a long learning process as the BEF transformed into a modern military capable of prosecuting total war. At times, though, the learning process would prove very difficult as some commanders demonstrated that they were incapable of achieving success in their new positions.

One of Haig's first actions upon elevation to command of the BEF was the creation of his own General Headquarters (GHQ) staff. That his command was not entirely independent quickly became apparent, for Haig wished to translate his staff wholesale from the First Army to their new positions at GHQ. However, Kitchener balked at the appointment of Major General R. H. K. Butler as chief of staff, and instead the position went to Lieutenant General Launcelot Kiggell, largely on the basis of seniority. Major General J. H. Davidson took over at Operations while Brigadier General John Charteris assumed control of Intelligence. Though the staff got along well, they were rather weak and singularly unsuited to stand up to their strong and demanding chief. While historian Gerard De Groot goes too far in referring to the staff at GHQ as, a "sycophantic . . . circle of simpering, awestruck admirers,"[5] severe problems certainly existed in the functioning of Haig's staff. Even John Terraine, Haig's leading supporter, contends that Kiggell, "never was, nor aspired to be, more than a mouthpiece for Haig."[6] Charteris, though reputed to be brilliant, was perhaps the most controversial of all. Rarely did the Intelligence chief report news that Haig would find distressing. Instead, Charteris constantly bombarded Haig with over-optimistic reports of an impending collapse of German morale. Based often on thin rumors, the reports had the effect of building up Haig in times of difficulty, leading him to believe that the constant application of more pressure would cause decisive victory.

Haig now had to develop his own style and personality both as the commander in chief of the BEF and as a leader of men. Serious in his belief, but never overtly spiritual, Haig turned to religion as the immensity of his present task became clear to him. Intrigued by the preaching of Reverend Dr. George Duncan, Haig appointed him de facto chaplain of GHQ, and attended service regularly. The spiritual messages were heartening, and Haig became convinced that God helped to guide him through the shoals and eddies of war. It was this religious surety of purpose that enabled Haig to persevere through horrific battles such at the Somme and Passchendaele. While some contend that Haig's religious belief only served to wrap his mistakes in a dangerous mantle of infallibility, Duncan himself disagrees, stating:

> Haig's faith was essentially practical. There is not the slightest evidence that he ever allowed it to pervert or overrule his military judgment. What it did for him was to give him an unshakable confidence in victory, a resolute will for victory, and a serenity which remained unclouded in the darkest hour.[7]

Haig often falls victim to the charge of being a "Chateau General," never leaving GHQ to investigate the conditions of the battlefront or to meet and congratulate the men who were fighting so hard for Britain. Born of reminiscences in postwar memoirs that were polemic in nature, the charges of Haig's isolation are in the main untrue. Though matters of command obviously kept Haig quite busy, he always took time to ride out to units stationed close by for inspections. As an example, in a two-week period in April 1916, Haig visited battalions of the Sixth Division, XIV Corps H.Q., Canadian and South African units, an RFC unit, and a sniping school; he also inspected base camps, hospital wards, recreation facilities, and a military prison.[8] Though Haig did not think it proper for the commander in chief to inspect the trenches during battle, he certainly was evident and active in his efforts to retain personal contact with his burgeoning military force.

Finally, Haig had to adopt a command relationship with his subordinate army commanders. Again the charge exists that dealings between Haig and his army commanders were singularly one-sided, with Tim Travers claiming that the "serious gaps in communication" between Haig and his army commanders were due in part to a fear among the commanders of questioning Haig's authority. There did, however, exist a weekly conference between Haig and his army commanders, at which strategic and tactical ideas were discussed. At first the meetings were certainly rather one-sided affairs. However, as the war went on the meetings became more open and productive. Haig also visited and liaised with individual army commanders, especially during the planning period before important offensives, often exhibiting startlingly varied approaches to command. Sometimes he would take a direct part in the planning and prosecution of an offensive, as in the Somme, and at other times he would remain rather distant and only offer advice, as in Third Ypres. Haig, though, did not view the differing command styles as inconsistent. Simply put, he sometimes believed the planning to be incorrect and chose to intervene on the tactical level, and sometimes not.[9]

Even as his command structure and style slowly developed, Haig turned to ideas of strategy and to the vexing question of how best to achieve victory in the Great War. Haig's guiding principle remained that the war had to be won through the defeat of the main German field army on the western front. He was joined in that conviction by Robertson, now Chief of the Imperial General Staff. Though the two had major differences, Robertson being more of a supporter of an attritional struggle rather than a breakthrough attempt, the two men made common cause against their foes, becoming one of the most important and influential military partnerships in British history. Upon his assumption of office Robertson was quite dismayed at the disorganized state of governmental relations with the military, reporting to Haig in January that the politicians, "have no idea how war must be conducted in order to be given a reasonable chance of success, and they will not allow professionals a free hand."[10] Most disturbing to Robertson was the fact that several leading political figures again pressed for operations in the east. Robertson had witnessed how the split between Kitchener and French had lessened the voice of the military in such debates, and was determined to make common cause with Haig. Though not overawed by Haig, Robertson chose his battles with the commander of the BEF carefully, often subsuming his own desires to the greater military good. Thus, though their relationship was far from perfect, Robertson and Haig worked together to present united opinions on military policy to the government.[11] Initially their alliance was overwhelming and achieved great success.

Haig also had to deal with the important question of his relations with his French allies, and soon received guidance in the form of a letter of instruction from Kitchener. The letter stated:

> The defeat of the enemy by the combined Allied Armies must always be regarded as the primary object for which the British troops were originally sent to France, and to achieve that end, the closest cooperation of French and British as a united Army must be the governing policy; but I wish you distinctly to understand that your command is an independent one, and that you will in no case come under the orders of any Allied General further than the necessary cooperation with our Allies above referred to.[12]

The document was thus quite mixed, urging Haig to cooperate with the French but reminding him that his command remained independent and going on to caution Haig against risking defeat in favor of French policy. For his part Haig would do his utmost to work in tandem with the French, though he remained skeptical about their ability to prosecute a prolonged war and assumed that more and more of the fighting would fall to the BEF. He wrote regarding his conclusions to Kiggell:

> In the past there has certainly existed on the part of the French a feeling that we were not always willing to take our fair share. No

doubt that feeling has existed on our side also. There must be a give and take. The present moment (with the change in command) is opportune for creating a good impression and paving the way for smooth negotiations with the French, especially as important matters in regard to combined operations are pending.[13]

Thus Haig chose to work closely with the French, and though relations were not always good, for the time being he chose to subsume his own operational planning to their strategic design.

Though battles with the politicians and negotiations with the French loomed, Haig and Robertson had made clear that the decision would come on the western front. But the question remained: What form was the ongoing war to take? Strategically Haig returned to his Staff College roots, advocating a series of "wearing out" attacks designed to draw in and destroy German reserves. He argued that these attacks should take place simultaneously and continuously from France straight through to Russia so that the Germans would not be able to use their interior lines of communication. Only after the Germans were on their heels would the Allies shift toward decisive battle on the western front. Thus Haig supported a series of "bite and hold" attacks geared toward creating the opportunity for decisive action. Haig, though, could not foretell the fact that both the German nation and military would prove resilient, capable of withstanding the rigors of total war. The opportunity for decisive battle, then, would not come in months as Haig hoped, but only after years of attrition.

Unable to pierce the veil of the future at the Chantilly Conference in December 1915, Haig and Joffre agreed to carry out their series of wearing-out offensives, to be followed by a major French effort at decisive battle. As part of the attritional process Joffre made it known that he favored an attack at the junction of the French and British armies near the River Somme. Haig, though, returned to the idea of operations along the Belgian coast in cooperation with the Royal Navy. It was Haig's opinion that an assault in the area of the Somme would seize only worthless territory, while a successful attack in Flanders would be valuable in a myriad of ways. A minor success there would seize important high ground, easing the lives of the British defenders of Ypres while also achieving the attritional goal. However, it was also an area where a more substantial victory seemed to beckon. Strategically Flanders represented a major German logistic bottleneck, and Haig believed that seizure of the communications hub of Roulers, some twenty-five miles distant, could even force a German evacuation of the valuable Belgian ports of Ostende and Zeebrugge—achieving one of the main strategic British goals of the entire war. In addition the German seaborne flank lay open to the possibility of an amphibious operation designed to exploit any success.

After receiving Joffre's reluctant assent, Haig hoped to launch his assault in the spring. However, on February 21, Falkenhayen preempted all Allied planning by launching a massive assault on Verdun. Falkenhayen hoped by this attritional offensive to "bleed the French army white" at Verdun, forcing an end to the war. Lasting ten months and causing nearly one million casualties, the Battle of Verdun is perhaps the signature battle of the Great War. The German offensive very nearly achieved its goal, leaving the French military and indeed the French nation battered and weakened. At first Haig did not realize the scope of the assault, but soon he began to turn his efforts to the aid of his stricken ally.

Though Haig, because of Joffre's entreaties, was only a recent convert to the idea of attacking on the Somme, he quickly became fully committed to the offensive. Greatly worried that the French were being pressed beyond the limits of their endurance at Verdun, Haig determined that his effort on the Somme had to be made with the maximum strength. Additionally Haig had reason for renewed optimism regarding the outcome of the coming assault, for the ongoing fighting at Verdun had also placed great strains upon the German army, and thus served as the "wearing down" battle dictated by Allied strategy. As a result Haig hoped that his Somme offensive would become the decisive battle, which would break the German lines and restore a war of movement. Intelligence received from Charteris also buoyed Haig's spirits. Though the German defenses were strong, Charteris placed great faith in reports of sagging German morale both on the battlefront and the homefront. Haig did temper his expectations through a realization that the coming offensive might only achieve an attritional aim, but he hoped that a substantial victory might injure German morale even further, possibly resulting in peace as early as the coming winter.[14]

Haig also had reason for optimism in that the BEF now had nearly attained the weight of infantry and artillery that he felt was necessary to achieve a decisive success. In addition he hoped that many of the command difficulties experienced at Neuve Chapelle and Loos were a thing of the past, and accordingly Haig turned over planning for the Somme to his most experienced subordinate, Rawlinson, who now commanded the Fourth Army. It must be remembered, however, that neither Haig and Rawlinson, nor their subordinate corps and division commanders, were properly prepared for what was to come. Staff College had not looked past a BEF of six divisions, leaving a poorly trained officer class to make ready for an attack of unprecedented size.[15]

Rawlinson quickly discovered that the German defenses in the area were quite formidable, consisting of two main trench systems and incorporating several fortified villages including Fricourt, Thiepval, and Beaumont Hamel. Rawlinson chose to advocate a methodical, "bite and hold" offensive scheme. He proposed that after a five-day bombardment the infantry advance on an attack frontage of 20,000 yards to seize only the German frontline trench system. After a delay of three days the attack would be renewed to seize the German second line of defenses. Rawlinson realized that his advocacy of a methodical advance went against Haig's thinking and he wrote in his diary: "I daresay I shall have a tussle with him over the limited objective for I hear he is inclined to favour the unlimited with the chance of breaking the German line."[16]

Indeed Rawlinson's draft plan did not receive the support of GHQ. Haig, favoring a shorter bombardment, instructed Rawlinson to amend his plan and to aim for greater goals, namely the seizure of both German lines of defense in one operation followed by a push eastward toward Combles. In addition Haig instructed Rawlinson to extend the front of the attack southward to the junction with the French army, and to have the cavalry on hand to exploit any favorable development. Haig realized that aiming for distant objectives on a broad front entailed great risk to the BEF, but argued that the time was right and, given the French predicament at Verdun, the risk was worth taking. Though not without misgivings, Rawlinson conformed to Haig's new design, and the goals for the Somme came to include an overthrow of both the German first- and second-line trench systems and an advance toward a newly discovered third line of defenses. Rawlinson did, however, persevere regarding the nature of the bombardment, which remained scheduled for five days duration.

The planning for the opening of the offensive at the Somme is perhaps the most controversial element in the entirety of Haig's tenure in command of the BEF, and the disaster that ensued still colors perceptions of his career. Strategically, in the main, Haig was correct. A British assault was indeed required to take pressure off the French at Verdun. As regards the goals for the Somme, Haig was certainly over-optimistic, but that failing can be understood. Germany had already taken severe losses that seemed to justify optimism. Possessing what he believed to be overwhelming strength and facing weakened German resistance, Haig hoped to build on the experience of 1915. Thus Haig's desire to achieve a breakthrough can be seen as a justifiable, if tragic, miscalculation based on evidence accumulated through the near success of Neuve Chapelle and Loos.

Tactically the team of Haig and Rawlinson made a series of errors, again based in part on an erroneous understanding of lessons from previous offensive actions. The infantry was rather poorly trained and lacked weaponry to facilitate its own advance at the Somme. Also, though the infantry did not universally advance to its doom in parade ground lines as is usually surmised, tactics were in the main poor and certainly not uniform. Rawlinson, with some seventeen infantry divisions at his disposal, did not impose a standard upon his subordinates, and thus in some cases the infantry advanced across no-man's-land in rushes, while in others the infantry received specific orders to advance only at a walk.

As in 1915, though, the bulk of the offensive would fall to the artillery, an awesome array of weaponry including 1,000 field guns, 233 howitzers, and 180 counter battery guns. The absolute numbers, though, are misleading, for the artillery was simply called upon to do too much with too little, having to destroy enemy wire, silence enemy artillery, and crush the entire enemy defensive network. The field guns dealt with enemy barbed wire and often failed in their task because of faulty ordnance and inaccurate fire. Though there had been advances in locating enemy artillery, the counter battery guns failed to subdue the 598 field guns and 246 howitzers that the Germans were able to bring into action. Finally, the main task of the offensive, destroying the German defenders themselves, fell to only 233 howitzers. Making matters worse, the German defenses in the area were very strong, including deep dugouts that were impervious to everything but a direct hit from a heavy caliber shell. Even against such defenses, a heavy weight of artillery fire, similar to that used at Neuve Chapelle, would have made seizure of the German frontline trench possible. Critically, though, Haig's decision to attack the German defenses in depth had the effect of diluting the overall effectiveness of the bombardment. Thus the fault for the impending disaster must fall to Haig, for it was as a consequence of his decision that "the British command decided to send its infantry against some of the strongest defenses on the western front in the wake of a preliminary bombardment approximately half as intense as that employed against the much sketchier German defenses at Neuve Chapelle."[17]

That Haig still had much to learn about the nature of the Great War is obvious, yet on the eve of the offensive he remained confident, noting in his diary:

With God's help; I feel hopeful. The men are in splendid spirits. Several have said that they have never before been so instructed and informed of the nature of the operation before them. The wire has never been so well cut, nor the Artillery preparation so thorough. I have seen personally all the Corps Commanders and one and all are full of confidence.[18]

Though it is outside the scope of this study to provide a detailed account of the Somme, the struggle forms a critical episode in Haig's conduct of the war, his growth as a commander, and his historical legacy. After a prolonged bombardment lasting seven days, during which a total of 1.5 million shells were fired at the German lines, on July 1, 1916, British troops made ready to go "over the top." Confidence was high, for it seemed that few Germans could have survived the tumult of the barrage. However, one million of the shells fired had been shrapnel designed only to cut the German wire, leaving only 500,000 shells of heavier caliber to do the bulk of the real work. Given the inaccuracy of the bombardment and recurring problems with shell fuses, the total was simply inadequate. Thus many Germans, though dazed and frightened, were quite alive and made ready to man their machine guns and to call down their defensive artillery fire.

After the explosion of a series of mines beneath the German lines, at 7:30 A.M. the infantry attack began. In the far north, a diversionary offensive launched by elements of the Third Army around Gommecourt met with very uneven success and in the end achieved little, struck by enfilade fire from unattacked German defenses. On the left flank of the main assault the VIII Corps also achieved minimal gain. Indicative of the unequal application of modern infantry tactics, though, some units, including the Thirty-sixth Ulster Divison, advanced into no-man's-land before the barrage had lifted and achieved the German front lines. However, the Thirty-sixth still lost heavily and was driven out of most of its gains before nightfall. Other units, though, did advance in slow-moving lines over great distances, and are perhaps best represented by the futile attack of the First Newfoundland Regiment. Finding their way forward to the front lines blocked by men and equipment, the Newfoundlanders clambered out of the trenches and fell victim to German fire before even reaching their starting point and lost some 91 percent of their attacking force with only a handful of men reaching the German frontline trenches.[19] Thus, though levels of success differed, in the main the story of the first day of the Somme north of the Bapaume Road is one of unremitting failure—thousands were lost, cut down in no-man's-land, with only a sliver of captured German trenches near Thiepval to show for their gallant effort.

South of the Bapaume Road, though, the situation was rather different, with the XV Corps and the XIII Corps achieving nearly all of their initial goals including the overthrow of the German first-line trenches in the area and the seizure of the defended villages of Mametz, Montauban, and Fricourt.[20] The reasons for success in the area are many, including better observation and adjustment of artillery fire, weaker German defenses, and one of the first British uses of the "creeping barrage," in which the infantry followed slowly advancing artillery fire very closely, hoping to reach the German trenches before their occupants could emerge. The French, cooperating on the southern flank of the British attack and aided by their considerable experience at Verdun, also achieved the vast majority of their initial objectives.

As the fortunes of the battle ebbed and flowed the communications realities of the Great War served only to worsen an already bad situation. At their respective headquarters Rawlinson and Haig slowly learned of the progress of the massive battle, but were in many ways powerless to alter the course of events. Rawlinson knew little of the failure in the north, or of the isolated successes in the area, until it was too late to send aid to units holding out in the German lines. More regrettably Rawlinson also knew relatively little of the success in the south. The Germans in the area were beaten, and local reserves were few. Through decisive use of reinforcements British forces could have

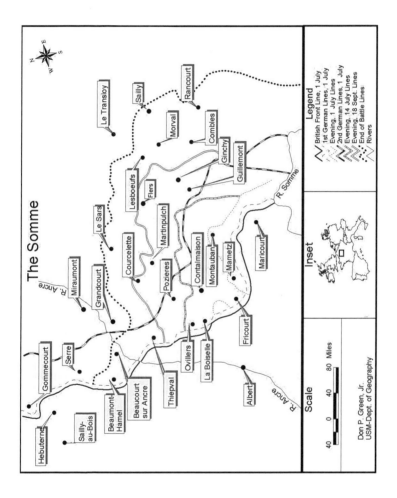

The Somme

Hebuterne

Sailly-au-Bois

Gommecourt

Serre

Beaumont-Hamel

Beaucourt sur Ancre

Thiepval

Ovillers

La Boiselle

Albert

R. Ancre

Miraumont

Grandcourt

Courcelette

Pozieres

Contalmaison

Montauban

Mametz

Maricourt

Fricourt

Le Sars

Martinpulch

Flers

Lesboeufs

Ginchy

Guillemont

Combles

Morval

Rancourt

Sailly

Le Transloy

R. Ancre

R. Somme

Inset

Scale

40   0   40   80 Miles

Don P. Green, Jr.
USM–Dept. of Geography

Legend

British Front Line, 1 July
1st German Lines, 1 July
Evening, 1 July Lines
2nd German Lines, 1 July
Evening, 14 July Lines
Evening, 18 Sept. Lines
End of Battle Lines
Rivers

at least taken the important areas around Trones and Mametz woods, which would be the scene of much bitter fighting in following months.[21] However, Rawlinson had not placed his reserve formations in a position to take advantage of the success, and as in earlier battles, an opportunity for greater advance was lost. In the words of historian Gary Sheffield:

> We know that by failing to capitalize on the success in the south the British commanders let an opportunity for a substantial advance go begging. Rawlinson never believed in Haig's plan for a breakthrough, and this probably influenced his reaction to events on XIII Corps' front. To lack any form of immediately deployable operational reserve was a mistake.[22]

At the cost of 57,000 casualties, the first day of the Battle of the Somme had fallen far short of Haig's considerable goals. The scale of the setback only slowly dawned upon Haig, who two days later still believed that the casualties numbered only 40,000. Even when he learned of the true nature of the losses incurred Haig never thought of calling off the offensive. After all, the strategic imperative that had led to the Somme still held firm, for the French still desperately required a continuation of the British offensive to lessen pressure on Verdun. Thus the Battle of the Somme would continue, but the severity of the losses, a national calamity for Britain, jolted Haig's optimistic belief in a breakthrough offensive.

Though follow-up operations continued Haig realized that the BEF needed a period of recuperation before launching another major offensive. Tension regarding the failure to advance ran rather high, and led to a heated exchange that helped to sort out the command relationship between the Western Allies. In a meeting on July 3, Joffre pressed Haig to continue the attack as soon as possible and argued that the BEF should strike in the northern sector of the battlefront toward Thiepval. Haig, however, advocated building on the successes of the battle through a further advance in the south toward Longueval with continuing French aid. Haig's diary records what happened next:

At this Joffre exploded in a fit of rage. '*He* could not approve of it.' He '*ordered* me to attack Thiepval and Pozieres.' If I attacked Longueval, I would be beaten, etc., etc. I waited calmly until he had finished. His breast heaved and his face flushed! . . . When Joffre got out of breath, I quietly explained what my position is relatively to him as the 'Generalissimo.' *I am solely responsible to the British Government for the action of the British Army*, and I had approved the plan.[23]

Thus Haig chose to delay a resumption of major offensive action, and stipulated that the renewed offensive would take place at the junction of the British and French armies south of the Bapaume Road. Haig's goals this time were far more modest, hoping only to seize the old German second line of trenches on a rather narrow frontage. Haig did stipulate, though, that Rawlinson's forces had to reach a proper jumping-off point for the coming assault. Mistakenly, Rawlinson turned the task over to his subordinates, resulting in some forty-six uncoordinated attacks against various German strong points in the area and some 25,000 additional casualties. Again the losses represent a failure for the command team of Haig and Rawlinson, for more sizable assaults with adequate artillery preparation could have achieved the same results at far less cost.

Rawlinson's plan for the coming major offensive demonstrated that both he and Haig had learned much from their earlier failures. The Fourth Army commander suggested that his forces advance into no-man's-land at night to facilitate a quick capture of the German frontline trench system. Haig initially disagreed with this portion of the plan, contending that tactical movement by night was as yet beyond the men of Kitchener's Army. Rawlinson and his subordinate commanders, though, pressed their case, and Haig relented. Thus the planning for the July 14 offensive represented a give-and-take, rather than the dictatorial approach usually ascribed to Haig, indicating that the commander in chief was also learning his role in modern combat. Sometimes, as before the first day on the Somme, he intervened in the planning of his subordinates; on other occasions he stood aside. In a very important sense, then, Haig's command style remained uneven and unpredictable, reflecting his confidence or lack thereof in the abilities of his subordinates.

That Rawlinson and Haig had embarked on a true "learning curve" is best demonstrated by the artillery plan for the coming battle. Though they had not developed a detailed formula for artillery success, and were not thus true scientific practitioners of modern war, Rawlinson and Haig did much to rectify the critical artillery deficiencies that had doomed the first day of the Somme offensive. For the coming attack, the Fourth Army could rely on support from 1,000 artillery pieces, of which 311 were heavy howitzers. Though there were 500 fewer artillery pieces than on the first day of the Somme, they were called upon to do much less. The attack frontage of July 14 was only 6,000 yards as opposed to over 20,000 yards on the first day of the battle. The supporting German trenches in the area of the assault amounted to only 12,000 additional yards, where there had been 300,000 additional yards of trenches on the first day of the battle. In essence, then, the artillery fire accompanying the attack of July 14 would be five times more intense than that on July 1, leading to a far greater level of destruction in the German defensive system.[24] Thus in the space of just two weeks Haig and Rawlinson had made significant alterations to their style of attack. Though communication would remain a nagging problem, both artillery and infantry tactics were much improved, as the results of the battle would indicate.

The British gained local surprise on July 14, by employing only a whirlwind bombardment followed five minutes later, at 3:25 A.M., by an infantry assault launched from prearranged positions in no-man's-land near the German lines. Everywhere the attackers met with great success, finding only smashed defensive works and dazed German soldiers, for the massive artillery barrage had done its job. Along the entire front the III, XV, and XII Corps reached their final objectives and overthrew what had been the German second line of defense, seizing Bazentin le Petit and Trones Wood. Once again a greater victory seemed to beckon, and Rawlinson attempted to utilize a cavalry advance to seize High Wood and the next belt of German defenses known as the Switch Line. Though the cavalry achieved initial gains, indicating a continued utility in warfare, it failed to achieve a sustained success against the German defenders of High Wood.[25] Though surprised, the Germans were using the realities of the Great War to their advantage by rushing reinforcements to the scene more quickly than the British could learn of and attempt to exploit any fleeting success. Nevertheless Rawlinson and Haig were rightly pleased and heartened by the victory. The BEF, inexperienced at all levels, had proven that it could defeat the talented Germans in battle, through the proper use of artillery support in an advanced all-arms battle.

The massive assaults of July had an immediate effect on German strategic thinking. Under Falkenhayen the Germans adhered to the idea of launching counterattacks to seize any lost ground. The German commander in the area of the Somme, General Fritz von Below, adhered to the defensive scheme, declaring that "the enemy should have to carve his way over heaps of corpses." To prosecute such an active defense, the Germans had to rely on lavish use of manpower and sent a total of forty-two extra divisions to the Somme area in July and August. Though in general the German defenders suffered fewer casualties than did their British and French attackers, the Germans lost their defensive advantage through launching some 330 counterattacks during the Battle of the Somme. Certainly Haig can be criticized for many of his decisions during the battle, but the vaunted Germans seemingly learned even more slowly, throwing away thousands of lives to recapture patches of shattered ground. Quickly the strain of battle began to show, and Falkenhayen decided on July 11 to suspend major offensive operations at Verdun. Though the struggle there would continue in the form of French counterattacks, the Battle of the Somme had achieved one of its prime strategic aims—pressure on the French army at Verdun had been relieved.

Though the crisis had eased, the French were very desirous

that the British attack continue lest the Germans once again seize the initiative. Haig also believed that only continuous pressure would eventually force the Germans into a position in which decisive battle would become possible. As an anxious nation began to realize the very difficult attritional nature of the Somme, Haig found himself having to defend the continuation of the offensive to the British government. Haig's response to the governmental inquiry is quite revealing. Haig contended that continued attrition would quickly use up the remaining German military reserves, and that the

> maintenance of a steady offensive pressure will result eventually in his complete overthrow. Principle on which we should act. *Maintain our offensive.* Our losses in July's fighting totaled about 120,000 more than they would have been had we not attacked. They cannot be regarded as sufficient to justify any anxiety as to our ability to continue the offensive. It is my intention:

> (a)   To maintain a steady pressure on Somme Battle.

> (b)   To push my attack strongly whenever and wherever the state of my preparations and the general situation make success sufficiently probable to justify me in doing so, but not otherwise.

> (c)   To secure against counter-attack each advantage gained and prepare thoroughly for each fresh advance.

> Proceeding this, I expect to be able to maintain the offensive well into the Autumn.[26]

Receiving continued governmental support, for the next two months, from July 15 to September 14 (sometimes dubbed the period of the forgotten battles) Rawlinson's Fourth Army and Gough's Reserve Army engaged in a continued series of small, often uncoordinated attacks to seize German defensive works in the areas near High Wood, Delville Wood, and Guillemont. The purpose of the continued struggle was to maintain pressure on the Germans through massive artillery attacks while seizing important defensive positions prior to the next main assault scheduled for September. During this period, the Fourth Army alone mounted some ninety operations, only four of which were launched across the entire front. In all during this period of "line straightening," the Fourth Army suffered 82,000 casualties while advancing only 1,000 yards on a five-mile front. Thus, while capturing less than the area seized in the more infamous first day of the Somme, the Fourth Army suffered 40 percent more casualties.[27]

Though the fighting during July and August was indecisive at best, Haig's characteristic stubborn optimism regarding the opportunity for decisive battle returned, fueled in part by Charteris's continued reports of sagging German morale on the battlefield and on the homefront. For his part Joffre, also subject to fits of great optimism, strongly advocated launching another major offensive on the scale of July 1, at the nexus of the French and British armies. Though there was considerable allied disagreement about the timing and goals of the coming campaign, eventually the effort was set for mid-September as a major advance in the neighborhood of Flers-Courcelette. Again much of the planning fell to Rawlinson, who devised a scheme for a limited advance. Haig, however, hoped for something much greater and remarked concerning Rawlinson's plan:

> In my opinion he is not making enough of the situation with the deterioration and all-round loss of morale of the enemy troops. I think we should make an attack as strong and as violent as possible, and plan to go as far as possible.[28]

As with the attack plan for July 1, Haig hoped to break three lines of German defenses in one continuous operation, to be followed by exploitation by five cavalry divisions husbanded behind the front lines. Haig's alteration of Rawlinson's plan had the effect of diluting the all-important covering artillery barrage, which now included creeping barrages as a matter of course, to a level of one-half of the intensity of the barrage accompanying the July 14 attack. Thus, though the BEF was becoming much better at firing accurate and effective barrages due to a period of "on-the-job training," Haig still struggled to find the optimum balance of artillery fire to accompany any major advance. Haig's confidence in success, though, was not based on levels of artillery fire, but on a stubborn and continuing belief that the Germans were nearing the end of their capability to resist. However, in the case of the coming attack Haig had an additional reason for optimism: the first battlefield use of the tank.

In many ways Winston Churchill was responsible for the early development of the tank, having recognized the need for an armored "land ship" to deal with enemy strong points. However, after Churchill's fall from grace following the Dardanelles adventure, the development of the tank fell into danger. Churchill, relegated to the western front, in late 1915 sent a variant of his planning to Haig, who expressed an immediate interest in the tank, thus ensuring its future as a weapons system. Though tanks were slow, mechanically unreliable, and only lightly armed, Haig realized the importance of the new weapon and placed an immediate order for 150 to accompany the initial Somme offensive.[29]

Haig's acceptance of the tank, when many other military leaders failed to appreciate its value, serves as the best proof that the British commander in chief was not the technophobe of popular portrayal. Indeed Haig's intervention at critical junctures was also instrumental in the development of the Royal Flying Corps, the Lewis light machine gun, the Mills grenade, and light and heavy trench mortars—all of which would play a major role in shifting the balance of warfare back toward the attacker. Perhaps Haig's advocacy of technology and his tireless persistence in acquiring the new weapons in abundance played a greater role in the coming successes of the BEF than his own tactical and strategic growth.

Tank production, though, proved slow, and the new weapon was not ready for the initial battles on the Somme. Haig, impressed by the prototypes he had seen in action, received word from Colonel E. D. Swinton, principally responsible for the later stages of the development of the tank, that at least seventy-five of the vehicles would be ready for the attack slated for mid-September. Swinton had earlier warned Haig not to use the tanks in "driblets," but to keep their existence secret until they could be used in large numbers in a great offensive.[30] Given his perceptions regarding the weakened nature of the German army on the Somme, Haig judged that seventy-five tanks would be sufficient to meet Swinton's requirements.

However, only forty-nine tanks reached France in time for the offensive, with only thirty-two reaching their eventual starting points for the assault. Very soon thereafter nine tanks broke down, and five became ditched, leaving only eighteen effectively in action.[31] Thus, when British and French forces moved forward to the attack on September 15, tanks were in effect used only in "driblets." Making matters worse, tank tactics were quite obviously in their infancy. Fearful that the tanks could not negotiate broken ground, Rawlinson arranged for gaps in the artillery barrage to allow the tanks forward. As a result British infantry, which outpaced even the few tanks on hand, often faced un-shelled German defenses, with predictably disastrous results, and few gains were made on the British right and left flanks. However, in the center of the British line, under the cover of a punishing barrage and accompanied by twelve tanks, British troops made notable advances, seizing the village of Flers and breaking the German second line of defenses. Though great gains had been taken in the center of the British line, again at high cost, a breakthrough did not beckon, and the cavalry remained in its billets. Even so the fighting continued in the area for two weeks as Haig and Rawlinson sought to press toward the third line of German trenches.

The success of the few tanks at Flers has brought Haig a torrent of criticism. David Lloyd George outlined the case against Haig in his *War Memoirs*:

> But the decision to launch the first handful of these machines . . . has always appeared to me to have been a foolish blunder. . . . We made the same error as the Germans committed in April, 1915, when by their initial use of poison gas on a small sector alone, they gave away the secret of a new and deadly form of attack, which, had it been used for the first time on a grand scale, might have produced results of a decisive character. . . . So the great secret was sold for the battered ruin of a little hamlet on the Somme, which was not worth capturing.[32]

More recent historical accounts, though, vindicate Haig for his early use of the tank. He had tried to amass as many of the machines as possible and hoped that their addition to the battle would result in a favorable decision. The tank was not yet a war-winning weapon, and even its massed use would not have achieved total victory on the Somme, as evidenced by later, fuller uses of armor at Cambrai and Amiens. The tank did, though, require a battlefield test to assure its worth and continued development. Even so, many within the British military considered the tank a failure; thus Haig's continued support of the weapons system remained critical to the further development of armor and armored theory. Haig followed the mixed debut of the tank with an order for one thousand more and encouraged the growth of a new branch of the army to deal with the new weapons system. Haig was thus far ahead of his time, hoping to add larger and more independent tank formations to his attack program for the coming year.[33]

Fighting on the Somme lingered until mid-November, making more use of bite and hold techniques. That Haig chose to continue the fighting for so long after hope for a major victory had dimmed is central to the criticism of his command. As the weather worsened, the Fourth Army and Reserve Army fought a series of bloody battles along the Ancre River and near the Le Transloy Ridge, culminating in the seizure of Beaumont Hamel—one of the initial goals for the first day of the offensive—on November 14, after over four months of fighting. Certainly Haig's decision to continue the struggle was due in part to his stubborn and optimistic nature. He remained true to the idea of a wearing-out struggle that had to be continuous in nature. He also firmly believed, based in part on Falkenhayen's failure at First Ypres, that the time for a decision might be near and that relaxing pressure on the German lines would be a critical mistake. Finally, Haig chose to continue the battle at the behest of the French, who, as the senior alliance partner, continued to demand attritional offensive action on the western front.

The Somme, quite possibly the most important battle ever in British military history, had come to an end. Though the rate of losses dropped considerably after the first day of the offensive, the eventual toll of the battle in death and suffering remained staggeringly high. British forces suffered 420,000 casualties, and the French lost 205,000 while together they succeeded in making only a dent in the German lines some thirty miles long and seven miles deep at its deepest point. The legendary futility of the offensive is best represented by the fact that the BEF had not succeeded in gaining all of the objectives set for the very first day of the assault. German losses in the Battle of the Somme remain quite controversial, but number between 500,000 and 600,000 casualties. The question remains, though, was the battle worth the effort and extreme sacrifice?

It is popularly accepted today that the Somme was a national cataclysm for Britain, representing the death of a generation of the nation's best and brightest at the behest of an uncaring and bungling high command. The case is encapsulated in the words of military correspondent Lovat Fraser:

> Our High Command had not advanced beyond the tactics of the Stone Age. They had not conceived any form of warfare except the blind fighting of masses of docile men against formidable positions month after month.[34]

Recently, though, historians have come to question the typical assumptions concerning the Somme. This revisionist school of thought, while not discounting Haig's many mistakes, has come to see the Somme as a costly yet pivotal victory for Britain and an indispensable step in the ongoing learning curve of the BEF.

During late August the Germans had replaced Falkenhayen with the command team of General Paul von Hindenburg and his First Quartermaster General Erich Ludendorff. The two men realized that the twin strains of Verdun and the Somme had placed an unacceptable burden on the German military system. Thus Ludendorff chose to recast German defensive tactics in the west in a fundamental way. First, the Germans abandoned the idea of fighting for every inch of ground, instead choosing to rely on a more elastic system of defense. Second, the Germans made plans to withdraw from much of the salient in central France to a prepared position that became known as the Hindenburg Line. In essence Ludendorff questioned the German ability to withstand another round of attrition and in his own words backed Haig's ongoing assumptions when he warned the German leadership to:

> bear in mind that the enemy's great superiority in men and matériel would be even more painfully felt in 1917 than in 1916. They had to face the danger that 'Somme fighting' would soon break out at various points on our fronts, and that even our troops would not be able to withstand such attacks indefinitely, especially if the enemy gave us no time to rest and for the accumulation of matériel.[35]

As a result of the fighting on the Somme, then, the Germans would not only retreat to the Hindenburg Line, but would also be willing to gamble on any chance for victory in the war. One such gamble involved the use of unrestricted submarine warfare, designed to destroy Britain, but destined to fail and cause American entry into the conflict. Thus the attritional victory of the Somme should be seen as an essential step along the path to eventual overall victory in 1918.

What remains is to assess the nature of Haig's leadership at the Somme. Certainly the commander in chief expected far too much from several of his major attacks, hoping to achieve a breakthrough victory. Haig also demonstrated a variable command style, sometimes intervening and meddling, and sometimes standing aloof even as mistakes were made. In addition, Haig allowed the battle to continue for far too long once the hope for a major advance had passed. Finally, and most disturbingly perhaps, Haig and Rawlinson both often failed to realize the lessons of artillery use during the offensive. Tragically, in many ways these mistakes can be ascribed to an untried commander in chief, leading a new army into the uncharted waters of modern war. In the words of Gary Sheffield:

In retrospect, it was unrealistic to expect the amateur and inexperienced BEF of 1916 to do much more than this, although clearly it could have performed more effectively at the tactical and operational levels.[36]

Thus the Somme was not the great victory that ended the war. Neither was it, though, the fruitless catastrophe of recent historical memory. Haig had bungled the offensive badly at times, but his command gaffes are understandable given an objective view of the context of his mistakes. Buoyed by a confidence that the Somme had been a success, and spurred by his religious faith and recurring optimism, Haig now prepared for another year of warfare. As usual he was convinced that during the coming year, if the Allies remained on the offensive, the German army would reach the end of its tether. That Haig had taken some of the wrong lessons from the battles of 1915 was evident. What lessons would he now take from the Somme to aid in the prosecution of subsequent offensives?

Chapter 5

Battles in the Mud: The Year of Passchendaele

I N THE WAKE of the decidedly mixed results of the Battle of the Somme, during November Haig and Joffre met in Chantilly and agreed on the need to keep continuous pressure on the German lines in France and Flanders, and that the first offensive of the coming year would be, in the main, a British affair. Haig, though his hope for an immediate decisive battle had dimmed, decided to use the opportunity to launch his long-desired attack in Flanders. At the same time events at sea served to focus the attention of a reluctant government on Haig's planning.

With an overstretched merchant fleet, and having lost control of much of the Belgian coastline, Britain's wartime supply line was vulnerable to attack. Making matters much worse, the Germans were threatening to launch their burgeoning U-boat fleet on a potentially devastating unrestricted campaign against British trade. Facing the threat of German attack, Arthur Balfour, the First Lord of the Admiralty, responded in November:

Of all the problems which the Admiralty have to consider, no doubt the most formidable and most embarrassing is that raised by submarine attack on merchant vessels. No conclusive answer has yet been discovered to this mode of warfare; perhaps no conclusive answer will ever be found.[1]

Reports from the Admiralty to the Asquith government were quite gloomy, some even predicting imminent defeat if the Germans chose to strike with their entire submarine fleet. With no naval means as yet by which to destroy submarines, on November 21 Asquith decided to advocate a ground assault aimed at seizing the German submarine bases at Ostende and Zeebrugge on the Belgian coast. Informing Robertson and Haig that, "the submarine constitutes by far the most dangerous menace to the Allies at the present," Asquith went on to instruct:

> There is no operation of war to which the War Committee would attach greater importance than the successful occupation, or at least the deprivation to the enemy, of Ostende and especially Zeebrugge.[2]

Haig took the wishes of his government to Joffre, who in December agreed that a British offensive in Flanders would form the first stage in the Allied offensive scheme for the coming year.

During December, though, discontented with Asquith's indecisive wartime leadership, a coalition of Liberal, Conservative, and Labour members took control of the House of Commons and elevated David Lloyd George to the position of prime minister, posing great problems for Haig. The two men were often at odds; Lloyd George did not trust Haig in the least, while the commander in chief thought the new Prime Minister to be "shifty and unreliable."[3] Most importantly, though, Lloyd George had always strongly favored shifting Britain's military might away from the western front to other, possibly more profitable, theaters of war. As such, Lloyd George's continuing devotion to the "easterner" school of thought ran contrary to Haig's unwavering belief that the might of the German army had to be destroyed in France and Flanders.

The strategic situation became even more muddled as Joffre fell from military power in France, eventually replaced by General Robert Nivelle, one of the heroes of Verdun. While an advocate of continued action on the western front, Nivelle favored his own plan for a massive, decisive assault on the German lines in central France over Haig's proposed Flanders scheme. Nivelle, unlike Haig a glib conversationalist and quite comfortable in the company of politicians, moved quickly to press his scheme on the reluctant British Prime Minister. Proposing a massive attack on a narrow frontage, preceded by the heaviest artillery bombardment in the history of warfare, Nivelle promised a decisive victory and pledged to call a halt to his offensive within two days if it showed signs of failure. To Lloyd George the plan was irresistible, for it promised a victory in which the French would pay the greatest cost.

Lloyd George had fallen under the spell of Nivelle's charm, and in writing to his mistress Frances Stevenson made clear his preference for Nivelle over Haig, stating: "Nivelle has proved himself to be a Man at Verdun; and when you get a Man against one who has not proved himself, why, you back the Man!"[4] Not knowing the extent of his fall into disfavor, Haig made ready to undertake the main British portion of Nivelle's plan, a diversionary assault near Arras, even as Lloyd George decided that the time was right to demonstrate his full authority over the military in matters of strategy and tactics.

Following discussions with the French and with members of the British War Cabinet, Lloyd George decided to use the occasion of an upcoming conference at Calais regarding transportation difficulties to make his stand. Oblivious to the secret machinations, Haig and Robertson attended the February conference, which opened with little fanfare. However, in meetings on the twenty-sixth Lloyd George dropped his bombshell by unveiling plans to restructure the system of command on the western front. Sir Maurice Hankey, the War Cabinet Secretary, recalled that the plan:

> fairly took my breath away, as it practically demanded the placing of the British army under Nivelle; the appointment of a British 'Chief

of Staff' to Nivelle, who had powers practically eliminating Haig as his Chief of the General Staff, the scheme reducing Haig to a cypher.[5]

Thus Lloyd George sought effectively to replace Haig, whom he did not consider a "clever man," with Nivelle.

Shocked and doubtless hurt by Lloyd George's actions, Haig and Robertson retreated to their lodgings to discuss their options. Haig recorded their decisions in his diary:

> We agreed that we would rather be tried by court-martial than betray the Army by agreeing to its being placed under the French. Robertson agreed that we must resign rather than be partners in this transaction. And so we went to bed, thoroughly disgusted with our Government and the politicians.[6]

The next day tempers flared, threatening a breakdown of the conference and the resignation of much of the command structure of the BEF. Hankey, though, worked hard to defuse the very tense situation and suggested that Haig be placed under Nivelle's direct command only for the duration of the coming offensive. Reluctantly all agreed to the compromise, and disaster was averted. Though Lloyd George had failed to supplant or remove Haig, the results of the conference had strained the already poor communications and faith between the Prime Minister and the commander in chief. Thus as the war neared a point of great crisis, relations between the government and the military in Britain were clouded by mistrust and animosity.

Now subordinate to Nivelle's planning, Haig made ready for the BEF's part in the offensive, calling for a British attack at Arras, followed by a massive French assault on the Chemin des Dames. Nivelle hoped that a French breakthrough would dislocate the German defensive system in central France and restore a war of movement. Once again, though, the Germans preempted Allied planning, this time by evacuating the salient they held between Arras and Soissons and retreating to prepared defensive positions known as the Hindenburg Line. The move shortened the German defensive network, allowed for the accumulation of much-needed reserves, and thoroughly disrupted Nivelle's planning, convincing

Haig that the French plan stood little chance of success. Again he turned to the idea of an attack further north, in part due to the worsening of the submarine war. However, Nivelle remained firm in his resolve, and thus the BEF made ready for a battle that lacked its full support and was not of its choosing.

The planning for the Battle of Arras, falling mainly to the First Army under General Sir Henry Horne, and the Third Army under General Sir Edmund Allenby, demonstrated that the BEF had learned much in its trials at the Somme. Especially for the assault against the powerful defenses of the Vimy Ridge, great care had been taken in the all-important artillery plan of battle. The exact length of trench to be assailed had been calculated, and the appropriate artillery assigned to the task at hand. The attacking infantry, also making use of more advanced tactics, were to be preceded not only by a creeping barrage, but also by a further barrage of machine gun bullets and light howitzer shells. In all the moving barrage was 500 yards in depth, and provided the advancing infantry with a great deal of protection. Also counter battery work had become more productive due to scientific advances in gunnery. Observation and communication had also improved. Finally, though, the application of sheer numbers told the true story. The attacking forces had gathered together some 2,827 guns, of which 863 were of heavy caliber. Thus the artillery barrage that accompanied the Arras attack was three times as strong as that employed on the first day of the Somme, in addition to being much more accurate and lethal.[7]

The infantry moved forward on April 9, to mixed results. While making only minimal gains on the right flank, in the center the Third Army tore a gap in the German lines and advanced over three miles, the greatest single forward movement since the onset of trench warfare. The opportunity again, though, proved fleeting. The Germans quickly rushed reinforcements to the scene and strengthened their failing defenses. Conversely, it was very difficult for the BEF to move artillery forward to replicate the detailed preparations that had enabled them to achieve their tactical success.

While the BEF had achieved measured success at Arras, Nivelle could make no such claim for his long-awaited offensive launched between Soissons and Reims, as French goals had proven wildly optimistic. Instead of halting the attack as promised, though, Nivelle pressed onward, seizing part of the Chemin des Dames Ridge in over two weeks of fighting at a cost of 180,000 casualties. The failure to achieve victory brought the shaky morale of the French army to a new low and resulted in a debilitating series of mutinies. The growing crisis led to Nivelle's replacement in command by General Philippe Petain and threw the remainder of Allied planning for the year into a state of disarray.

Convinced of the need to attack the German lines and hoping to forestall any offensive against the weakened French, Haig returned to the idea of an attack in Flanders toward the Belgian coast. Haig realized, though, that gaining the support of Lloyd George for such an offensive would be quite difficult. However, the Germans had unleashed their submarine force with devastating results, in April alone sinking 847,000 tons of shipping. Such losses were unsustainable and forced the First Sea Lord, Admiral Sir John Jellicoe, to advise the government that the war would soon be lost unless an answer could be found quickly,[8] giving Haig's planning a needed boost.

After a conference with Lloyd George and French leaders in Paris, Haig received preliminary support for maintaining the offensive on the western front. With the new authority Haig went on to plan an offensive in Flanders that was both varied and flawed. In a conference with his army commanders on May 7 Haig announced that his offensive would take place in two phases. First a subsidiary attack scheduled for June would seize the dominating high ground flanking the main offensive at Messines. Next a force from Ypres would attack, with the goal "to regain the Belgian coast up to the Dutch frontier, or, failing this, to dominate the Belgian ports now in the hands of the enemy."[9] The conclusion that Haig still dared hope for a decisive breakthrough offensive in the face of all available experience is unavoidable. However, discussions with subordinates would serve to temper Haig's optimism.

To lead his most cherished offensive, Haig chose General Sir Hubert Gough, who knew little regarding the terrain of the Ypres salient. A much more obvious choice was General Sir Herbert Plumer, a methodical commander who was very familiar with the area of the offensive. Haig, though, chose Gough in the vain hope that he would be better suited to seize any fleeting opportunities for the reinstitution of mobile warfare. In the end Haig's choice of Gough would prove to be one of the worst mistakes of his tenure in command of the BEF.

The experience of Arras, which had dragged on for six weeks at an eventual cost of 150,000 casualties, forced Haig to expect less from his coming offensive at Ypres. In late May Kiggell, Haig's chief of staff, wrote to Gough concerning the new German defense in depth system. He informed Gough that the Germans relied on a weakly held front line of strong points that could give each other mutual support. The first waves of British attackers would penetrate these lines only to face massive German counterattacks in the German second line of defenses known as the battle zone. Thus Kiggell counseled Gough to aim only for limited advances,[10] leading Haig to his final plan for the Flanders offensive, which would take the form of a methodical series of bite and hold attacks. Disturbingly, though, Haig continued to hope that the sum total of attacks would lead to a collapse in German morale.

Haig entrusted the preliminary stage of his Flanders offensive to the Second Army of Plumer. Laboring on a plan for an attack there since January, Plumer responded with a masterpiece framework for a limited offensive aimed at the seizure of the Messines-Wytschaete Ridge. As with the earlier assault at Arras, Plumer carefully calculated the amount of artillery fire needed to overcome the German defenses in the area. Again Haig complicated matters by suggesting more comprehensive objectives, but Plumer in the main stood firm against the wishes of his chief. As a final part of his planning Plumer oversaw the construction of several tunnels dug beneath the German lines, containing over one million pounds of explosives.

At 3:10 A.M. on June 7, the explosion of nineteen mines punctuated the devastating British bombardment. Only six hours later Plumer's infantry had seized the ridge, having met little resistance and suffered few losses. The fighting at Messines continued for a week as the Second Army consolidated after having reached all of its limited goals. Messines, following in the wake of Arras, indicated that the BEF was becoming much more proficient at warfare. In both cases, using lavish artillery fire, the British had been able to achieve an effective break into the German defensive system. Exploitation of the gains, though, had remained impossible. The victories had given Haig great confidence in the rising abilities of the BEF, but it was a confidence tempered by realization of the need to aim for limited goals.

Even as the Battle of Messines raged, though, Lloyd George stepped back from his support of Haig's overall planning. The Prime Minister, seeking to streamline wartime government, created the War Policy Committee, which included himself, General Jan Christian Smuts, Lord Milner, and Lord Curzon. The committee, which began its deliberations on June 11, took a fresh look at Britain's strategic options for 1917, and Lloyd George, noting Haig's unwavering optimism, let it be known that he favored operations in Italy over a continuation of Haig's plan for an offensive in Flanders. Robertson immediately took note of the danger that the committee represented to operations on the western front and wrote to Haig expressing his desire to present a united military front to the politicians. Haig responded to Robertson's entreaties by crafting a memorandum that outlined his revised hopes for a continuation of the Flanders campaign. The memorandum presented the offensive as a series of bite and hold operations aimed at achieving both tactical goals and attrition. Haig, though, continued to believe that German morale was nearing the breaking point and revealed his continued hope for more decisive results by stating:

It is my considered opinion, based not on mere optimism, but on a thorough study of the situation, guided by experience which I may claim to be considerable, that if our resources are concentrated in France to the fullest possible extent the British Armies are capable and can be relied on to effect great results this summer—results which will make final victory more assured and which may even bring it within reach this year.[11]

Robertson did not agree with Haig's assessment of the situation regarding the state of German morale and pressed Haig to keep his optimism in check. To ensure the future of the Flanders plan the two men had to be united in their support of the operation when dealing with the committee. Thus Robertson warned Haig:

What I do wish to impress on you is this—Don't argue that you can finish the war this year, or that the German is already beaten. Argue that your plan is the best plan—as it is—that no other would be safe let alone decisive, and then leave them to reject your advice and mine. They dare not do that.[12]

On June 19, Haig journeyed to London and, together with Robertson, placed the details of his Flanders plan before the War Policy Committee. The two men worked hard to show that short, attritional advances would greatly ease the situation of the BEF at Ypres. In addition they contended that if great results did accrue, the Belgian coast would be lost to the Germans. Lloyd George vehemently protested that the BEF lacked the ability to achieve such a victory and that the necessary French aid was not likely to be forthcoming. At the end of the meeting indecision reigned, and the committee was evenly split on the matter. On the next day, though, Jellicoe appeared before the committee, again stressing that the war against the submarine was being lost and throwing his weight behind Haig's proposals.[13]

On June 25 Lloyd George and the War Policy Committee, barely a month before the onset of the offensive, reluctantly gave their assent to Haig's planning. The scheme had very nearly been ruined by Haig's continued optimism, but had been rescued by the strength of the alliance between Haig and Robertson. Only the unanimity of military opinion, including that of Jellicoe, made the Third Battle of Ypres possible. Lloyd George, who in the end had the ultimate authority over military actions, planned to keep a close eye on the progress of the offensive and on the commander in chief.

In the planning for his second major offensive on the western front, Haig demonstrated a style of command quite different from that seen on the Somme. Instead of altering the planning for Third Ypres, Haig stood more aloof and was satisfied only to give advice and general strategic oversight to the planning of Gough. Doubtless Haig believed in Gough's ability, as the entire BEF had become more professional and needed less oversight. In addition, as historian Tim Travers has demonstrated, Haig preferred a "hands off" style of command, leaving tactical issues to the commander on the scene.[14] This rather loose command style, preferred in modern militaries, relies upon high and uniform levels of training and tactical ability on the battlefield. Allowing Plumer such initiative would have worked well, but Haig had chosen the wrong commander. Gough would prove intransigent and unwilling to follow Haig's admittedly over-complicated directions and goals.

As Gough began his planning he continued to receive warnings from Haig and Kiggell regarding the nature of the German defenses and of the need for only short advances. In addition Haig warned Gough to concentrate his efforts against the Observatory Ridge and Gheluvelt Plateau on the right flank of the offensive. German defenses in the area were considerable; the ground dominated the battlefield and if unconquered would enable the Germans to enfilade British forces further to the north.[15] Instead of heeding the advice, Gough produced a plan that spread his forces rather evenly across the battlefield and called for his men to advance as far as possible. In many ways it was the first day of the Somme in reverse. Haig and GHQ advised limited attacks and the concentration of artillery fire. The commander on the scene, though, wanted much more and thus chose to disperse the all-important artillery cover.

Certainly the BEF aimed at goals that were beyond its means at the opening of the Third Battle of Ypres. The plan to rush through to distant objectives as at the Somme, though, was part of Gough's tactical scheme. Haig retained hope that a strategic victory would be forthcoming, but planned to gain that victory through sustained limited advances. It was thus a complicated and mixed message that Haig sent to his subordinate. The result was a breakdown in command at the highest levels of the BEF. Haig and Gough were at cross-purposes, a situation fraught with danger and one that Haig should have taken in hand but did not. After the war, in a letter to Sir James Edmonds, the British official historian of the war, Gough made clear the command difficulties preceding Third Ypres:

> Put briefly, the main matter of difference was whether there should be a limited and defined objective or an undefined one. G.H.Q. favoured the former, I the latter. My principal reason was that I always had in mind the examples of many operations which had achieved much less than they might have done, owing to excessive caution. . . . In all these operations victorious troops were halted at a pre-arranged line at the moment when the enemy was completely disorganized . . . this was the argument which I used, I claim with complete justification, with Douglas Haig.[16]

On July 16, the preliminary bombardment began for the Third Battle of Ypres, often mistakenly referred to as Passchendaele. Though Gough had assembled 752 heavy and 1,422 field guns, the bombardment varied in effectiveness due in part to the effort to advance to depth and partly to bad weather.[17] Making matters worse, Gough did not concentrate adequate levels of artillery fire against the heavily defended ridge system on the British right flank. Thus Gough's planning had not been as meticulous as that at Arras and Messines, which led to widely varied results on the battlefield.

On the left flank French forces achieved their goals with relative ease, while the British XIV Corps captured the Pilkem

Ridge and advanced to a depth of 3,000 yards. In the center the XIX Corps achieved the greatest advance, pushing beyond the German third line of defense. On the all-important right flank, however, the three divisions assaulting the Gheluvelt Plateau met with little success. The German system of elastic defense allowed for a measure of British forward movement, but the gains, especially in the center, were still notable. The situation worsened, though, as enfilade fire from the plateau, combined with German counterattacks, drove the XIX Corps from its forward positions. At the end of the day British gains totaled eighteen square miles of territory at the cost of 27,000 casualties. The results, then, were much greater than those on the first day of the Somme but failed to bear out the promise evidenced by Arras and Messines and certainly failed to achieve any of Gough's greater goals.

Though Haig expressed in his diary that he was pleased with the efforts of his troops, he was not at all happy with the way that Gough's attack had unfolded. In the ensuing days Haig again appealed to Gough to place more emphasis on the Gheluvelt Plateau, and a memorandum from Kiggell bluntly warned Gough not to attempt advances beyond 2,000 yards. Kiggell again informed Gough regarding the nature of the German defensive system and advised limited advances that did not outrun artillery support before facing the inevitable German counterattacks.[18]

Gough did not bother to respond to Kiggell's critique of his offensive scheme, and instead continued with his plans for deep penetration of the German lines. On August 10, after a delay caused by deteriorating weather conditions, which transformed much of the low-lying and shell-torn land of Flanders into a bog, II Corps launched an attack on the Gheluvelt Plateau. Gough, though, had failed to concentrate his artillery on the German positions, and the attack achieved little. The failure should have caused Gough to postpone his next attempt at the German center, but he did not relent. As a result the Fifth Army assaulted all along its front on August 16 with results very similar to that of the first day of the offensive. On the left considerable gains were made, but in the center and on the right the advance came to grief amid a maze of German concrete pillboxes and through German counterattacks.

Haig remained unhappy with Gough's handling of the offensive. Since May, Haig and his staff had been warning Gough regarding the need for limited advance and concentrated military effort on the Gheluvelt Plateau, only to be ignored. As a result Haig took what was, for him, an extraordinary step. By August 26, he transferred the capture of Gheluvelt Plateau to Plumer's Second Army, and made that the focus of his continued offensive. Gough remained involved in the fighting, in command of forces on the British left. Haig, however, had finally made good his critical mistake and placed the command of the battle in the hands of Plumer, who would adhere to a step-by-step approach of limited offensives. The first phase of the Third Battle of Ypres had come to an end.

Unlike Gough, who selected geographic goals and tried to make his firepower fit the plan, Plumer calculated the power of the infantry and artillery at his disposal and then established the limit of his advance. In his first assault, the Battle of the Menin Road, the Second and Fifth Armies attacked on a narrow frontage, used more advanced infantry tactics, and hoped to penetrate the German lines only to a depth of 1,500 yards. The weight of shell available to cover the advance was three times that fired during Gough's initial offensive. Finally, the plan called for British forces to halt their advance well within the range of their artillery to await and defeat the inevitable German counterattacks.[19]

On September 20, Australia/New Zealand Army Corps (ANZAC) and British troops went over the top, and within a few hours had achieved nearly all of their objectives. Surprised by the shallow nature of the British advance, the Germans held their counterattack forces too far back, and in the evening failed in their attempts to retake lost territory. At a cost of just over twenty thousand casualties the BEF had achieved nearly all of its

Painting of Sir Douglas Haig. *Courtesy of Mary Evans Picture Library*

Portrait of Field Marshal Sir Douglas Haig on horseback. *Courtesy of the National Archives and Records Administration*

Lt. Gen. Sir Henry Rawlinson, architect of Neuve Chapelle, the Somme and much of the Hundred Days. *Courtesy of the National Archives and Records Administration*

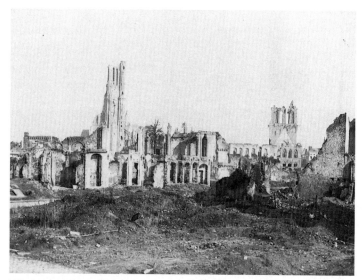

The tortured remains of the once beautiful city of Ypres, site of three major battles in the Great War, in November 1916. *Courtesy of the National Archives and Records Administration*

Mud and desolation during the latter phases of the Battle of the Somme. Though Passchendaele became synonymous with bottomless mud, the Somme also at times became nearly impassable. *Courtesy of the National Archives and Records Administration*

Early British tank stuck in a trench. Tanks were not yet the war-winning weapons that they would become in World War II. The slow speed and mechanical unreliability of the tank, in tandem with the fact that tank tactics were in their infancy, left the Great War controlled in the main by artillery and the machine gun. *Courtesy of the National Archives and Records Administration*

The trail of mud and desolation near Broodseinde in November 1917 during the Third Battle of Ypres. It was this third phase of the battle that gave Passchendaele its reputation for horror and futility.
Courtesy of the National Archives and Records Administration

Three of Haig's top subordinates, left to right, General Sir Herbert Plumer, the victor of Messines and the architect of the second phase of the Third Battle of Ypres; General Sir Edmund Allenby, who commanded the Third Army at the Battle of Arras; and General Sir Henry Horne, who commanded the First Army during Arras. *Courtesy of the National Archives and Records Administration*

Cartoon from the cover of the April 14, 1918, issue of the German magazine *Kladderadatsch* depicting Hindenburg thrashing Haig during the German offensive. The German celebration, though, was premature as both Haig and the BEF would survive to play the greatest role in the defeat of the German army in 1918. *Courtesy of Mary Evans Picture Library*

The Menin Gate in Ypres, on which are carved the names of the 54,896 officers and men of the commonwealth forces who died in the Ypres Salient area and who have no known graves. *Courtesy of Kathy Barbier*

The Thiepval Memorial, which contains the names of 73,357 British and South African men who have no known grave and who fell on the Somme between July 1916 and March 1918. *Courtesy of Andrew Wiest*

Headstone to fallen members of the Newfoundland Regiment and the Border Regiment at Y Ravine Cemetery on the Somme. Note that two soldiers were often marked on the same headstone with their unit badges as carved at the top. British and commonwealth families were able to add personalized final messages to their fallen loved ones, as Lance Corporal Pike's did. It reads "Be ashamed to die until you have gained some victory for humanity." *Courtesy of Terry Whittington*

British cemetery on the Somme. *Courtesy of Andrew Wiest*

Remains of the British frontline trench at Beaumont Hamel. *Courtesy of Terry Whittington*

Remains of a British trench near Ypres. *Courtesy of Kathy Barbier*

The Cenotaph in Whitehall, London. The monument to Britain's World War I dead. *Courtesy of Jill Wiest*

Haig's statue, a block away and directly facing the Cenotaph in Whitehall, London. Some have suggested that the statue be removed due to its proximity to the Cenotaph. *Courtesy of Andrew Wiest*

admittedly limited goals and had seized much of the strategic high ground around Ypres. The first effort at a step-by-step advance had been a resounding, if costly, success. With his optimism buoyed, Haig agreed with Plumer that the next step in the plan should take place without delay.

At dawn on September 26, again following careful artillery preparation, BEF forces advanced into the Battle of Polygon Wood. Along a short attack frontage the Second and Fifth Armies again achieved most of their goals and succeeded in destroying German counterattacks at a cost of just over fifteen thousand casualties. Though the price was high and the gains limited, Haig became convinced that the step-by-step approach was wearing down the Germans and portended greater results. Revealingly, Haig advised Plumer and Gough not to underestimate the decline in German morale. Haig then referred back to one of his formative moments in the war and pointed out that Falkenhayen had failed to press his advantage at First Ypres. Advising against a similar mistake, Haig recommended having reserve forces on hand, including cavalry, to exploit any opportunity.[20]

On October 4, Plumer launched his third attack, the Battle of Broodseinde. Though the fighting was more difficult, in part because of the limited time available for artillery preparation, the Second and Fifth Armies again seized most of their final objectives. Worried regarding the ongoing fighting, the Germans had chosen to place a higher number of troops in the front lines to contest the forward zone with more vigor. The move was a mistake, allowing a greater number of Germans to fall victim to the still effective artillery barrage. Thus Plumer's force, aided by tanks, advanced over 1,000 yards and seized five thousand rather demoralized German prisoners of war. The positive results, in tandem with Charteris's ever-optimistic reports regarding the imminent failure of German morale, once again convinced Haig that decisive battle was possible.

Haig advised Plumer to continue the hammer blows on the German lines without delay, hoping that finally the limited advances would lead to the ultimate breaking of the German lines

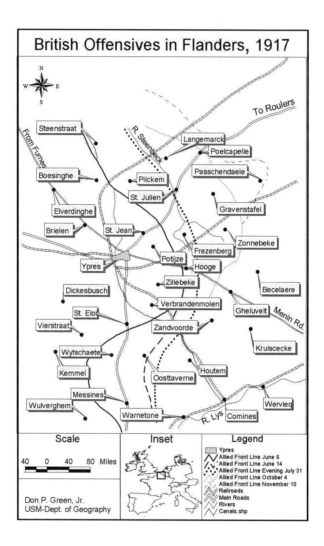

British Offensives in Flanders, 1917

To Roulers

Steenstraat

From Furnes

R. Steenbeck

Langemarck

Poelcapelle

Boesinghe

Pilckem

Passchendaele

St. Julien

Elverdinghe

Gravenstafel

Brielen

St. Jean

Zonnebeke

Frezenberg

Potijze

Ypres

Hooge

Zillebeke

Dickesbusch

Becelaere

Verbrandenmolen

St. Eloi

Gheluvelt

Menin Rd.

Vierstraat

Zandvoorde

Wytschaete

Kruiscecke

Kemmel

Houtem

Oosttaverne

Messines

Wulverghem

Wervicq

Warnetone

Comines

R. Lys

Scale	Inset	Legend

40 0 40 80 Miles

Ypres
Allied Front Line June 6
Allied Front Line June 14
Allied Front Line Evening July 31
Allied Front Line October 4
Allied Front Line November 10
Railroads
Main Roads
Rivers
Canals.shp

Don P. Green, Jr.
USM-Dept. of Geography

and an advance even to the Belgian coast where an amphibious landing would turn the German flank. However, at the same time the weather in Flanders, which had been fine during Plumer's victories, broke, and the rain began to fall. The landscape turned to a sea of mud and desolation, making military maneuvers nearly impossible. As a result both Plumer and Gough informed Haig that they would welcome a closing of the campaign. It was an important moment in Haig's career. If he had chosen to halt the offensive, Third Ypres would be remembered as a costly victory in which the BEF had overcome initial problems in command to win a series of important victories over mighty German defenses. Instead Haig chose to fight on as the weather worsened. As at the Somme the continuation of the offensive was in the main a mistake, brought on at least in part by a misplaced optimism that continued pressure would force German morale to collapse. As a result Third Ypres would become known as Passchendaele in reference to the last, tortured phase of the campaign. The continued progress indicated by the middle portion of the battle would largely be ignored, leaving Passchendaele to be remembered for futility, horror, and bottomless mud.

On October 9, Plumer's force made little headway in the Battle of Poelcappelle. The worsening weather made artillery preparation difficult, and the rushed nature of the attack allowed little time for readjustment. In an effort to keep nearly continuous pressure on the Germans, Haig had seemingly forgotten the need for meticulous preparation and planning that was the only way forward in the Great War. Only two days later the attack was renewed, aiming at an advance of 2,000 yards and the seizure of Passchendaele Village. With so little time to prepare, forced to slog through gripping mud and facing imposing German defensive works, the First Battle of Passchendaele also achieved but little, at the cost of a further thirteen thousand casualties. Allowing the attack to proceed at all had been a mistake, and pressing for two attacks in such quick succession in such conditions had been a critical error. Though recent historical interpretations suggest that the state of the German army after months of sacrifice in Flanders actually warranted optimism,[21] Haig's continuation of the battle would forever scar his reputation. Obviously the commander in chief was far from infallible and though he had made significant advances, he still had much to learn about the nature of the Great War.

The Third Battle of Ypres ended anticlimactically. Haig relented in his desire for great gains, and the Canadian Corps launched a series of very limited attacks aimed at the seizure of Passchendaele and part of the surrounding ridgeline. Struggling through the nightmare landscape, the Canadians forged ahead and on November 10 captured Passchendaele, heralding an end to the campaign. On the surface the results of Third Ypres closely mirror those of the Somme; at a cost of some 250,000 casualties the BEF had failed even to reach all of the goals that Gough had set for the first day of his campaign. However, on closer inspection Third Ypres can be considered a costly victory and an important step on the learning curve.

The offensive had done great service by not allowing the Germans to launch an attack on the beleaguered French in 1917. German casualties were also high, contributing to the attrition process, the ultimate German inability to achieve victory in their offensives of 1918 and the final German collapse by the end of that year.[22] In a tactical sense during 1917 the BEF had shown itself to be a much improved military force. At Arras, Messines, and during the central stage of Third Ypres the BEF had used tactics far in advance of those seen at the Somme and proved adept at defeating the most powerful German defenses in bite and hold offensives.

What remains is to gauge Haig's performance during Third Ypres. Without doubt Haig had chosen the wrong commander for the first phase of the offensive. Though Haig often advised Gough regarding the need for a step-by-step advance, his hand had not been firm enough and had allowed control of the battle to slip away, in part due to Haig's own enduring optimism. Too slowly, perhaps, Haig corrected his mistake by shifting to

Plumer and the tactics that had proven so successful at Messines. The ensuing limited victories, though, caused Haig to seek greater results, thus eschewing the very methodical tactics that had made Plumer's victories possible.

Thus the record of Haig's command at Third Ypres is decidedly mixed, and included valuable steps forward blended with significant errors in judgment. Haig had made mistakes in his prosecution of the Somme, but his errors in that battle could in part be forgiven because it was his first major battle as commander of the BEF. After Passchendaele, however, Haig would receive no such absolution. The enduring perception of failure and futility would forever tarnish Haig's career. In 1935 an article in the *News Chronicle* said in relation to Haig's reputation:

> Why has not Haig been recognized as one of England's great generals? Why, as a national figure, did he count for less than Lord Roberts, whose wars were picnics by comparison? The answer may be given in one word—Passchendaele.[23]

There remained, however, a considerable postscript to the fighting and political maneuvering of 1917—a battle that indicated the way forward in warfare, but that also illustrated the continuing imperfections in the evolving command of Douglas Haig. That battle was Cambrai. Since its introduction at the Somme, the tank had played subsidiary roles in later battles including Arras and Third Ypres. However, tanks had remained unreliable, few in number and of only marginal use in the great trench battles of the year. As improved models of the tank appeared, though, Brigadier General Hugh Elles, the Tank Corps commandant, and his senior staff officer Colonel J. F. C. Fuller, began to press for an opportunity to use tanks in large numbers over more suitable terrain. As early as September, the idea had caught Haig's attention, as had the separate planning by the Third Army, under the command of General Sir Julian Byng, for an offensive action toward Cambrai.[24] German defenses in the area were weak and the Third Army plan of attack was both novel and impressive. Haig and Kiggell were intrigued, but thought that operations at Ypres would deny Byng needed reinforcements. By mid-October, though, the two ideas for attack had melded into one, and Haig came to the conclusion that Byng would have enough men, tanks, and matériel to achieve at least a limited victory; he thus gave the plan his blessing.

At dawn on November 20, some three hundred tanks led five infantry divisions of the Third Army's III and IV Corps forward into the attack. Though armor was quite important to the overall plan, Haig rightly believed the tank to be only an ancillary weapon at this point. Indeed, the most innovative part of the Battle of Cambrai involved the artillery, augmented by the actions of the Royal Flying Corps acting in a ground attack role. In previous battles artillery barrages had often been long in duration and had always required extensive preregistration fire. However, at Cambrai the Third Army, for the first time, relied on "predicted fire," using better maps and calibration of artillery rather than preregistration to achieve accuracy. Thus the attack caught the two defending German divisions totally by surprise, a far cry from the opening day on the Somme just over a year earlier.

The attack quickly rumbled through the first and second defensive networks of the vaunted Hindenburg Line and was only checked outside Flesquières where tank/infantry cooperation was inadequate. Even so the results of the offensive were unprecedented, with troops advancing over four miles in places, something that had not been achieved in four months of fighting at Third Ypres. The results, though, were far from perfect. On the left flank little progress had been made against German defenders on the dominating high ground near Bourlon. Also, several tanks were lost to both enemy fire and to malfunctions. Lacking a method of communication, the remaining tanks quickly lost their operational cohesion. Finally, Haig once again had a mixed plan going into the battle. While a tactical advance toward Cambrai with a corresponding shock to the German defensive network would reap an attritional advantage, Haig also had the cavalry on hand in an attempt to exploit any greater victory. The cavalry did move forward, but after achieving initial gains failed to pierce the final lines of German resistance. With no other available reserves, weakened as the BEF was from Third Ypres, there remained little Haig could do to further his initial victory.[25]

Though the preconditions for success were now gone and the units engaged in battle under-strength and tired, Haig pressed his offensive for a further seven days, mainly in an effort to capture the Bourlon Ridge to make the pronounced salient gained by the attack less vulnerable.[26] By November 27, the offensive ground to a halt and the tanks began to leave the battlefield to regroup. In Britain there had been great celebration of the victory, with the ringing of church bells for the first time since the onset of the war. However, the celebration was premature as the Germans quickly gathered reinforcements for a massive counterattack.

Only the IV Corps in the northern part of the salient noticed the German preparations and made ready, while forces in the other portion of the salient remained in an offensive posture. The failure must fall in part to Byng, but resides mainly with Haig, who later took full responsibility for the resulting setback. On November 30, the Germans struck, also employing new offensive techniques involving the use of highly trained storm troopers. The surprise attack pushed the British from nearly all of their previous gains and only faltered after tanks from the Second Tank Brigade returned to the battle. Haig's great victory had turned, at best, into a costly draw.

The setback at Cambrai, which had started with such optimism, very nearly brought Haig's military career to an abrupt end. Lloyd George had approved offensive action by the BEF on the western front in 1917 only with great reluctance. As Third Ypres ground slowly on, with little in the way of territorial gain, the Prime Minister became less and less patient with Haig, Robertson, and the command structure of the BEF. As the prospects for victory in Flanders dwindled, Lloyd George and the

War Cabinet brought considerable criticism to bear on Robertson and Haig, focusing on the over-optimistic projections that had preceded the offensive. Lloyd George continued to cast about for other military options, such as offensive action in Palestine, but in the end limited himself to sniping at Haig from the sidelines. In the end Lloyd George could have ended the Flanders offensive that he would later pillory in his *War Memoirs*, but he did not. In the words of Robin Prior and Trevor Wilson:

> There is a terrible omission here. None of Lloyd George or Smuts or Curzon or Milner or Bonar Law seemed to be noticing that the Flanders campaign was his responsibility. It would continue not another day if they denied it authorization. . . . The most the nation's civilian rulers might do regarding it [Third Ypres] was wring their hands and look about for additional military advisors to offer a 'second opinion.' . . . So as the rain fell in Flanders and thousands of Haig's soldiers prepared to struggle through mud to their doom, the Prime Minister who was proclaiming the futility of this undertaking failed to raise a finger to stop it.[27]

In the wake of the German counterattack at Cambrai, though, the military situation suddenly changed and Lloyd George, who had never trusted Haig's optimism, now had to face the prospect of Haig's pessimism. With the end of the war in Russia, Haig contended that the Germans would quickly shift their forces westward and seize the initiative. As a result Haig and Robertson pressed the government to send all available troops to the western front to redress a predicted increasing imbalance in manpower. The shift in strategic fortunes galvanized Lloyd George to action, and a letter from Robertson served to warn Haig of the coming storm:

> His [Lloyd George's] great argument is that you have for long said that the Germans are well on the down-grade in morale and numbers and that you advised attacking them though some 30 Divisions should come from Russia; and yet only a few Divisions have come, and you are hard put to it to hold your own! He claims that five Divisions [that the government had directed sent] to Italy and absence of necessary drafts are not sufficient to account for the Cambrai

events, but that the latter are due to Charteris's error of judgment as to the numbers and efficiency of German troops.[28]

Thus as 1917 drew to a close Haig faced the prospect of a German offensive on the western front, while fighting for his life as commander in chief of the BEF.

Chapter 6

1918: The Year of Victory

FIELD MARSHAL SIR DOUGLAS HAIG looked forward to the coming of the new year with some trepidation. The collapse of Russia enabled the Germans to shift considerable forces to the western front, seizing the advantage over the Allies who were still attempting to recover from their offensive exertions of 1917. As a result, Haig, for the first time in the war counseled a shift to a defensive posture in France and Flanders. Though Haig's expectations regarding the nature of the coming German offensive varied, he remained confident that the Allies would hold firm as had the Germans at the Somme and Passchendaele.

Lloyd George, though, was quite skeptical regarding Haig's intentions, and became convinced of the immediate need to lessen the power of Haig and Robertson over strategy. In essence the Prime Minister moved to take control of the war away from the "westerners," with a goal of shifting British power away from France and Flanders to other, hopefully more profitable, theaters of war. Realizing that Haig and Robertson remained powerful, and that any overt move to oust them would endanger his government, Lloyd George chose rather indirect methods of achieving his goals.

The first move that Lloyd George made to reduce the power of Robertson and Haig during October 1917 was toward the construction of an Allied general staff, which initially took the form of an advisory body known as the Supreme War Council. By this means the Prime Minister hoped to place his ally General Sir Henry Wilson on the Allied general staff and into an advisory position roughly comparable to that of Robertson. In the words of David Woodward:

> With his man Wilson as a member of the Allied general staff, he [Lloyd George] hoped to have two sets of military opinion from which to select. Never again would he occupy the impossible position he had found himself in during the Passchendaele debate. Then it had been his amateur strategy against the monolithic military bloc, with Haig, Robertson, and Jellicoe all speaking with one voice.[1]

Continuing his efforts to lessen Haig's authority, Lloyd George moved against the more vulnerable members of Haig's inner circle of advisors. On December 7 Lord Derby, the Secretary of State for War, wrote to Haig stating that the War Cabinet had lost faith in Charteris as intelligence chief. Citing Charteris's consistently optimistic reports concerning German morale the memorandum informed Haig that, "the War Cabinet should have the fullest confidence in the opinions and judgments of officers of your Staff, and this they will not have so long as Charteris remains D.M.I."[2] Haig attempted to salvage Charteris's reputation by informing Derby:

> The responsibility for the judgment formed on the evidence obtained [from Charteris] and for the reviews put forward to the War Cabinet rest on me and not on him, and if the War Cabinet are not satisfied with the views put forward by me it is I, and not Charteris who should answer for these views."[3]

Haig eventually relented in his defense of Charteris, but the assault on Haig's staff did not abate. The next major figure to fall from grace was Kiggell, Haig's chief of staff, who was suffering from what was termed "nervous exhaustion." Though Haig admitted that he was "very sad to make this decision, especially when I reflect over all I and the whole Army owe to Kiggell," Haig did not object to his replacement.[4] In all, before the purge of Haig's staff was complete he had lost his director of intelligence, his chief of staff, his deputy chief of staff, his quartermaster general, his engineer-in-chief and his director-general of medical services. General Sir Herbert Lawrence moved into the position of chief of staff while Brigadier General E. W. Cox became intelligence chief. Haig did not struggle to the end in defense of his staff in part because he realized his political weakness, but also because he realized that the changes were needed to retain the faith of the War Cabinet in the actions of the British military. In total the changes to Haig's staff were needed and even John Terraine, Haig's staunchest defender, admits that the command shakeup actually strengthened GHQ and made Haig's command structure more secure and effective.

Even as controversy threatened British political and military unity, the continuing issue of manpower came to the forefront to cloud counsel even further. Dealing with depleted divisions and facing imminent German attack, the British military requested a force of 600,000 new men to keep British armies overseas up to their recommended establishments. However, the British government only allocated some 100,000 men to the task, placing the armed forces behind both shipping and agriculture in importance. Though the demands of the military were, in the end, unreasonable and impossible to meet were Britain to remain economically viable, Lloyd George seized upon the issue as yet another method of control over the military. The Prime Minister was playing a dangerous game, hoping to curb Haig's ability to prosecute offensive warfare by denying the military needed manpower—thus altering the nature of the conflict. In December 1917, Lloyd George had made his position clear in a communication to Lord Esher, "Now he [Haig] wrote of fresh offensives, and asked for men. He would get neither. He had eaten his cake, in spite of warnings. Petain had economized his."[5]

The twin controversies of manpower and control over British strategy joined at the January 30 meeting of the Supreme War Council, and focused even more attention on the issue of making the best use of available forces through the creation of an Allied general reserve. Haig, though he contended that he had no reserves for the creation of such a force, was greatly worried about the potential command structure of the Allied general reserve. He and Robertson suggested that the force be subject to the chiefs of staff of the British and French war offices, but Lloyd George had other ideas. The Prime Minister suggested that the Allied general reserve instead fall under the control of the military representatives to the Supreme War Council, Generals Ferdinand Foch and Wilson, placing the latter in a position to challenge Robertson as military adviser to the British government. As expected, Robertson decided to resist such a scheme at all costs. Haig, though, was more concerned with the alteration in the nature of the command system, and did not want to cede either his authority over his troops or his reserve forces to Allied control.[6]

Lloyd George returned home from the Supreme War Council having won a considerable victory. The Allies had chosen to stand on the defensive in the west and the military high command had been outmaneuvered over the issue of a general reserve. Though many of the details of the scheme remained to be decided, the Prime Minister had reason for optimism. However, Robertson continued to withhold his support and precipitated a controversy that nearly destroyed the government of David Lloyd George. Both Robertson and Lord Derby threatened to resign if the changes were implemented, and pressed Haig for support of their position. As Haig made his way to the center of the political fray, Lloyd George attempted a number of expedients to mollify Robertson and Derby, including sending Robertson to the Supreme War Council and moving Wilson to Chief of the Imperial General Staff (CIGS). In each scenario, though,

Robertson found that his power would be split with Wilson and thus remained adamant in his continued opposition.

On February 10, Haig arrived in London and learned of Lloyd George's desire to shift Robertson and Wilson. He received assurances that Robertson would be "free and unfettered" in the advice he would give, but would report to the government through Wilson. Though Haig doubtlessly realized that such an arrangement would lessen the power of his ally and friend, Robertson, and raise the power of Wilson, whom he distrusted, Haig decided that such an arrangement, though not perfect, was acceptable. Shocked by the reaction, Roberston pressed Haig for his support. Haig, however, responded, "this was no time for anyone to question where his services were to be given. It was his *duty* to go to . . . [the Supreme War Council] or anywhere else the Government wished it."[7] Haig had made the difficult, yet correct, decision to stand in support of governmental control of the war rather than fight in favor of his ally in matters of strategy, and after a further week of bitter controversy Robertson fell from power. Wilson took over as CIGS while Rawlinson took the position as the British representative at Versailles. One of the great personal alliances in British military history had come to an end.

After the bout of political infighting it remained to implement the new scheme of military and civilian control on the western front, and certain realities conspired to cause the ruination of the power of the Supreme War Council. In London Lloyd George and Wilson had achieved their aim of removing Robertson and seizing an added measure of influence over events. As a result their support for the machinery at Versailles and the issue of a general reserve lessened. For his part, Haig, though resigned to working under the flawed system, still did not favor placing British soldiers under a foreign commander and also argued that he could not spare forces for the formation of the general reserve. Haig found a staunch ally for his position in Petain, who also did not want to surrender control of his reserve forces. Thus with the Prime Minister satiated and unwilling to force another conflict with the military, the issue of the general reserve collapsed under the weight of the ongoing manpower crisis.

Predicting a British manpower shortage of 100,000 by June and facing an estimated total of 190 German divisions on the western front, Haig argued that he required all available units in the BEF to hold the line. Haig recorded on March 10:

> *The manpower situation is most unsatisfactory* . . . with heavy fighting in prospect, and very few men coming in, the prospects are bad. We are told that we can only expect 18,000 drafts in April! We are all right under normal conditions for men for the next three months, but I fear for the *autumn! And still more do I fear for the situation after the enemy has started the attack.*[8]

In total agreement, both Petain and Haig chose to abide by a personal pledge to send their own reserves to the other's aid in time of dire need. In the face of united military opinion Lloyd George chose not to press the issue, and the idea of raising a general reserve was shelved until the rising numbers of American troops once again made the idea feasible. Though he was not overly concerned with the failure to implement an effective system at Versailles, Wilson did lament the lack of a general reserve and proved prescient by remarking that Haig's actions had quashed the general reserve and that "he would have to live on Petain's charity [in case of an attack on the British lines], and he would find that very cold charity."[9]

While political turmoil swirled in London and Paris, Haig also had to make ready to deal with the strategic and tactical realities of facing the imminent German offensive. Haig remained quite confident in the defensive prowess of the BEF, but stark numbers serve to demonstrate the difficulty he would soon face—with some fifty-nine divisions (forty-seven British, ten Dominion, and two Portuguese) the BEF had to defend 126 miles of the western front while facing eighty-one German divisions, with a further twenty-five divisions held in central reserve. Haig correctly judged that the main weight of the German offensive would be directed against the BEF, and feared that the attack would fall in the north. In Flanders British and Allied forces enjoyed little in the way of strategic depth, and any substantial retreat would place them in danger of being cut off and destroyed. Haig also realized, though, that the German attack might fall at the juncture of the French and British armies further south. However, he rightly believed that the forces in that area (Gough's Fifth Army) could, in need, withdraw and rely on reserves promised by Petain before placing the communications hub of Amiens in danger. Thus Haig distributed his available forces accordingly from north to south: the Second Army with fourteen divisions defended twenty-three miles of front, the First Army with sixteen divisions defended thirty-three miles of front, the Third Army with sixteen divisions defended twenty-eight miles of front, while the Fifth Army with fourteen divisions defended forty-two miles of front.[10] Thus, though the defensive situation was far from perfect, and would bring much criticism down on Haig after the opening of the German offensive, his defensive dispositions were made on sound strategic principles.

After years of practicing offensive warfare, the BEF now had to ready itself for a defensive battle, and based on the considerable experience of assailing the German lines, Haig chose to advocate an elastic system of defense. At a conference of his army commanders Haig warned:

> Depth in defensive organization is of the first importance. . . . The economy of forces in the front line system is most important in order that as many men as possible may be available in reserve. The front line should generally be held as an outpost line covering the main line of resistance a few hundred yards in the rear.[11]

As a result, work on trench systems and the conversion to defense in depth proceeded apace, but made only slow progress, in part because of a critical lack of manpower for labor battalions. The situation was especially bad in the Fifth Army area, which had only recently been taken over from the French and was in a state of defensive disrepair.

Though Haig remained firm in his conviction that Flanders represented the most vulnerable part of the British line, evidence began to mount that the Germans would in fact strike first in the south against Gough. In February Haig warned the Fifth Army commander that any German attack would almost certainly break into the defenses of the BEF, and thus Gough should put much more effort into and reliance upon the preparation of his reserve lines.[12] As both Gough and Haig turned to the mounting prospect of a German attack against the Fifth Army, a dangerous disconnect developed. To face the coming storm Gough requested additional reserves and made ready to fight in a manner more reliant on forward defenses and manpower. Haig, though, had counseled defense in depth and even warned Gough that it might be impossible to mount large-scale counterattacks based on lavish use of manpower even in the battle zone of the defensive system. Indeed Haig argued that it might be necessary to engage in a fighting withdrawal to the area of Peronne on the Somme while awaiting promised French reserves to stall the German attack.[13]

Having made strategically sound decisions, as the German offensive neared, Haig confided to his wife, "I must say I feel quite confident, and so do my troops. Personally, I feel in the words of 2nd Chronicles, XX Chap., that it is 'God's battle' and I am not dismayed by the numbers of the enemy."[14] Haig's confidence, though, was soon to be tested, for on March 21, seventy-six German divisions struck at the Fifth Army between Arras and Laon in an attempt to drive a wedge between the British and the French. In addition to their obvious numerical advantage, the Germans employed effective, but in the end deeply flawed, tactics against Gough's imperfect system of defenses. Instead of using linear tactics to achieve fixed objectives, the Germans, aided by a thick fog, used storm-troop methods focusing on tactics of surprise, speed, and deep and continuous penetration. The German infantry worked to infiltrate and then bypass strong points, taking the path of least resistance. German artillery tactics were similarly inventive, relying on a short, intense barrage aimed more at harassing the enemy than achieving his destruction.[15]

In defense Gough had erred by placing too high a percentage of his men forward, in positions that were too distant from each other to offer needed support, and German attackers quickly penetrated into the Fifth Army's as-yet-incomplete battle zone. Thus, vastly outnumbered and poorly deployed, Gough's Fifth Army quickly began a retreat. At first Haig realized little of the nature of the setback, and believed the situation to be well in hand. By March 23, though, Haig had learned that the Fifth Army had failed in its efforts at defense in depth and in places had been pushed back more than twelve miles, confiding, "I was surprised to learn that his [Gough's] troops are now behind the Somme and the R. Tortville . . . I cannot make out why the Fifth Army has gone so far back without making some kind of stand."

In response to the German advance Haig attempted to secure the promised reserve forces from Petain, reminding the French commander that the Germans, if unchecked, could divide the Allied armies and drive the BEF into the sea. In a meeting on March 24, though, Haig discovered that the required reserves were not going to be forthcoming. Petain contended that the German attack was but a diversion, to be followed by an attack toward Paris, which would necessitate retention of French reserve units. Haig recorded, "I at once asked Petain if he meant to abandon my right flank. He nodded assent and added 'it is the only thing possible, if the enemy compelled the Allies to fall back still further.'" The refusal came as a true shock to Haig who continued, "In my opinion, our Army's existence in France depends on keeping the British and French Armies united."[16]

Haig faced a grave crisis partly of his own making. The Fifth Army, which had at best only poorly understood its role in the battle, was retreating under constant German pressure. BEF reserves were positioned too far to the north and faced a suspected second German attack in that sensitive area. The French reserves that had been earmarked to support Gough and make good his defense, though, were being withheld. In response, an Allied conference convened at Doullens on March 26, to deal with the growing crisis. Haig was quite certain that disaster would ensue if the French did not shift reserves to the defense of the Amiens area, and he did not believe Petain capable of such decisive action. Thus for the good of the Allied cause, and as a move toward gaining the needed reserves to avoid defeat, Haig put aside his national pride. At the conference Clemenceau suggested that Foch be placed in coordination of the Allied effort to defend Amiens. Haig recorded in his diary:

> This proposal seemed to me quite worthless as Foch would be in a subordinate position to Petain and myself. In my opinion, it was essential to success that Foch should control Petain; so I at once recommended that Foch should *co-ordinate the action of the Allied Armies on the Western front.* Both Governments agreed to this.[17]

Thus Haig was critical to the construction of a unified Allied command on the western front. Though it took some time to iron out the details of the arrangement, especially the level of Foch's control over British reserves, Haig had taken the critical step by sublimating his desires to the greater good. Simply put, Haig believed that Petain's pessimism had placed the Allies on the road to certain disaster. In an effort to control Petain and reclaim the situation Haig had been willing to elevate Foch to supreme command. Ironically, the move to place British forces under the supreme leadership of a foreign commander, so cherished by Lloyd George and hitherto consistently resisted by Haig, would serve only to strengthen Haig's hand. On most strategic issues Foch and Haig saw eye-to-eye, and Foch's leadership placed a buffer between Haig and his political tormentors in London. Thus supreme command would serve to blunt criticism of Haig, and would in many ways allow the commander in chief of the BEF a much freer hand in decision making than he had ever before enjoyed.

Even as the Allies moved toward a unified command, the German offensive began to stall. Though too much blame was attached to his command failings, and too little claim given to new German methods, Gough was replaced in command by Rawlinson. The change in commanders, though, was not critical to the battle, for shifting needed reserves to the area combined with the grim realities of the Great War to bring the German forward movement to a halt. The German forces had taken heavy losses, were tiring, had outrun their critical artillery support, and perhaps most importantly had outrun their own supply system.[18] Allied lines eventually held firm near Villers Bretonneux, and, though the Germans had succeeded in an advance of nearly twenty-five miles they had failed to take the critical rail junction of Amiens. The battle had been quite costly, with the BEF losing 175,000 casualties and the Germans suffering a roughly similar fate. Haig faced stern questions in London about his handling of the battle, and twice suggested that if the government did not trust his judgment it should replace him. However, even as the military and the government sparred over the blame for the setback, the Germans prepared to strike again.

Haig had long been certain that the Germans would launch their main attack further to the north, and as fighting died down near Amiens he pressed Foch for reserves to face the expected offensive. Foch, however, demurred even as the Germans attacked on April 9, between La Basse and Ypres. With a numerical advantage of two to one the Germans were able to achieve a five-kilometer advance toward the critical logistics hub of Hazebrouck. Realizing the serious nature of the attack, Foch agreed to move "a large force" of French soldiers to the north but declined to take over any part of the line to free British reserves for the battle. Understanding that a German advance to depth in Flanders would threaten the entire British war effort, Haig responded on April 11 by issuing a famous dispatch to his troops. Lauding their defensive efforts Haig went on:

> Many amongst us are now tired. To those I would say that victory will belong to the side which holds out longest. The French Army is moving rapidly and in great force to our support. There is no other course open to us but to fight it out! Every position must be held to the last man; there must be no retirement. With our backs to the wall, and believing in the justice of our cause, each one of us must fight on to the end. The safety of our homes and the freedom of mankind alike depend on the conduct of each one of us at this critical moment.[19]

The promised French reserves were slow in arriving, causing Haig great anxiety. However, much more quickly than before, the German offensive lost momentum. In Flanders the British defenses were much better prepared and dealt quite harshly with the German attackers. There remained moments of crisis, including the fall of Mount Kemmel and the need to evacuate the gains made in the hard-fought Third Ypres offensive of 1917. However, by the end of the month the German attack had slowed, and Haig noticed that "the enemy was not fighting with the same determination he showed at the beginning of the battle."[20]

The German attack in the north had stalled, but the overall cost had been great. The BEF had, in both German offensives, lost a total of 240,000 casualties. Already under-strength before the attacks, the manpower crisis now loomed larger than ever in the BEF. Lloyd George and the British government moved quickly to make good the losses, but not before controversy struck. As recriminations flew regarding the setbacks on the western front, General Sir Frederick Maurice, the Director of Military Operations on the Imperial General Staff, leveled a public accusation at Lloyd George of starving the BEF of troops. As the government fought through the dangerous controversy, Haig remained aloof from the struggle, writing to his wife, "Reuter states that Gen. Maurice has written to the papers. This is a grave mistake. No one can be both a soldier and a politician at the same time. We soldiers have to do our duty and keep silent, trusting to Ministers to protect us."[21]

On May 27, after a period of relative calm, the Germans struck again, this time against the French. As with the offensive in March the Germans made great initial gains and eventually penetrated the French lines to a depth of twenty-five miles, once again reaching the Marne River. At first Haig was quite reluctant to part with his own reserves to aid the French, fearing that the attack was a diversion to mask a later effort to be made against the BEF. However, as the situation continued to develop and worsen, Haig relented and Allied agreements codified the power of Foch as supreme commander over the movement of British units. The shift to a truly unified command was not made without animosity, but Haig agreed, and the German attack once again began to lose momentum.

Though the Germans continued to move forward into July, their pace had slowed considerably. Both Haig and Foch were now certain that the Germans would not win the war by military means in 1918, and the two began to consider mounting offensive operations of their own. After deciding first to launch a series of quite limited offensives, on July 4, ten battalions of Australians struck and seized Le Hamel. After a brief German offensive on July 15, the French launched a successful counterstroke on July 18, along the Aisne River. It now was readily apparent to both Haig and Foch that the tide on the western front had turned and that the time for a major Allied offensive was at hand. In London, though, the British government still despaired regarding the ongoing fighting, and Lloyd George hoped to wait for the arrival of massive American forces before launching any counterattack. However, though efforts to replace Haig continued, the Prime Minister's control over his commander in chief was lessened by the reality of Foch's supreme command. Regardless of Lloyd George's wishes, in a meeting on July 24, Haig and Foch came to the conclusion that the time was right for "regaining the initiative and passing to the offensive." The two agreed that the BEF would launch a surprise attack in the area of Amiens as soon as possible.

The planning for the initial major BEF offensive of 1918 fell once again to Rawlinson. Judging that the Germans around Amiens had done little to construct defensive works and were under strength, Rawlinson and Haig realized that speed was of the essence if they were to capitalize on the situation and thus took only three weeks to plan and prepare the coming offensive. Relying on elaborate measures to ensure secrecy, Rawlinson's draft scheme called for an attack by eleven divisions on a 19,000-yard front from Morlancourt to Demuin. The advance was to take place in three stages and aimed at British, Canadian, and

Australian forces penetrating the German lines to a depth of 6,000 yards, a mammoth goal considering the relative lack of forward movement in earlier British offensives. Haig approved Rawlinson's desire to achieve great goals at Amiens, and accepted Rawlinson's plan with little interference; in the words of Prior and Wilson:

> We may contrast this behavior with his [Haig's] attitude before and during the Somme campaign of 1916, when he intervened frequently and in detail during the planning process. No doubt in the aftermath of the Hamel operation he was more confident that the Fourth Army knew its business. But it was also the case that, as the British army at every level became a more complex, sophisticated, and above all specialist organization, any detailed intervention by the commander-in-chief became increasingly inappropriate. Haig's job . . . was—it may be suggested—diminishing not expanding as the forces under his direction grew in expertise and complexity. And Haig . . . proved far more effective as a commander once the sphere of his activities began to diminish to an extent that brought them within the limits of his capabilities.[22]

Indeed the British methods of attack were a far cry from what had been seen on the first day of the Somme only two years prior. Infantry, which had been outmatched in 1916, now packed a considerable punch allowing for greater tactical flexibility on the battlefield. In 1918 each British battalion had at its disposal thirty Lewis guns (portable machine guns), eight light trench mortars, and sixteen rifle-grenadiers. Thus the infantry now carried the firepower that effectively enabled it to deal with enemy strong points without having to wait for cumbersome artillery support. With their newfound strength the infantry was able to use speed and infiltration tactics to advance to depth. Additionally, the Fourth Army could rely on a force of over five hundred tanks and enjoyed command of the air during the coming battle.

Of the greatest importance, though, were advancements in the use of artillery. The weaponry at hand, 1,236 field guns and 677 heavy guns, had increased greatly in accuracy and lethality since the Somme. Also, with the newfound power of the infantry, the artillery was called upon to do less. There was no plan for the artillery to destroy the German trenches at Amiens; it only had to facilitate the advance of the infantry by keeping the Germans under cover. Still, the gunners relied on a strict ratio of weight of shell to enemy trench, leaving nothing to chance. Also, using techniques known as flash spotting and sound ranging, British artillery now proved quite adept at locating and silencing enemy artillery batteries. Thus during the coming attack British artillery effectively kept the Germans in their trenches and silenced their supporting guns, calming the deadly German "storm of steel" that had cost the lives of so many British attackers during 1916 and 1917. At the Battle of Amiens the Fourth Army demonstrated an unparalleled level of all arms coordination—aircraft, armor, infantry, and artillery all working seamlessly together—the true formula for tactical success in the Great War.[23]

With the aid of complete surprise the Fourth Army advanced in the early morning hours of August 8, under the cover of a heavy mist, achieving results that were remarkable in terms of the Great War. Except on the extreme flanks the Fourth Army reached all of its major goals, advancing up to eight miles, capturing four hundred enemy guns, inflicting fifteen thousand casualties on the defenders, and capturing twelve thousand prisoners while French forces captured some three thousand more. It was a truly prodigious victory, forcing Ludendorff to dub August 8 as, "a black day for the German Army in the history of this war."[24] The victory, due in part to the brave accomplishment of Dominion forces, heartened Haig, who recorded in his diary that, "the situation had developed more favourably for us than I, optimist though I am, had dared even to hope!"[25]

With Haig and Rawlinson expecting even greater results, possibly including cavalry action, the attack continued the next day, and though somewhat ragged in comparison, achieved an advance of a further three miles. However, the realities of the Great War now worked against the British as they had worked against the Germans in March. Attacking units had lost cohesion, tanks

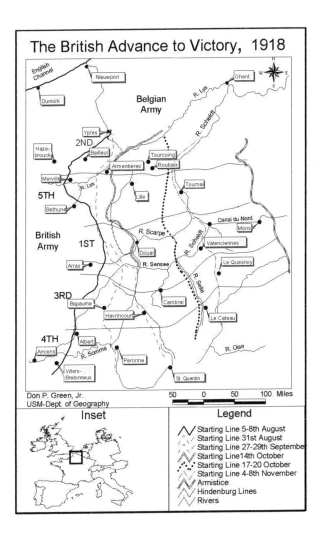

The British Advance to Victory, 1918

English Channel

Nieuwport

Dunkirk

Belgian Army

R. Lys

Ghent

R. Scheldt

N
W   E
S

Ypres

2ND

Haze-brouck

Bailleul

Tourcoing

Armentieres

Roubaix

Merville

R. Lys

5TH

Lille

Tournai

Bethune

Canal du Nord

Mons

British Army

1ST

R. Scarpe

R. Scheldt

Valenciennes

Douai

Le Quesnoy

Arras

R. Sensee

R. Selle

3RD

Bapaume

Cambrai

Havrincourt

Le Cateau

4TH

Albert

R. Somme

R. Oise

Amiens

Peronne

Villers-Bretonneux

St. Quentin

Don P. Green, Jr.
USM-Dept. of Geography

50   0   50   100   Miles

Inset

Legend

/\/ Starting Line 5-8th August
Starting Line 31st August
Starting Line 27-29th September
Starting Line14th October
Starting Line 17-20 October
Starting Line 4-8th November
Armistice
Hindenburg Lines
Rivers

had broken down in droves, and communications had suffered terribly. Most importantly, though, the British had advanced so quickly as to outrun their critical and overwhelming artillery support. In contrast, the Germans had rushed reinforcements, both men and guns, to the battle area. The balance of warfare, earlier tipped by detailed planning and overwhelming firepower, had shifted back to the defender. In previous such situations Haig had chosen to fight on in an attritional style, but such was not to be the case in 1918.

After only four days of fighting Haig and Rawlinson called an end to the Battle of Amiens. At first Haig wanted to call only a short halt to allow the Fourth Army a chance to regroup. However, the Commander of the Canadian Corps, Lieutenant General Sir Arthur Currie, informed Rawlinson and Haig that he believed the continuation of the offensive to be a "desperate enterprise," given the shifting balance of forces. Haig listened to his subordinate and called off a further attack in the area in favor of widening the offensive to include the First and Third Armies. In a meeting on August 14, Haig informed Foch of his intentions, eliciting an angry reply from the Supreme Commander tantamount to an order to continue the offensive. Haig recorded in his diary, "I spoke to Foch quite straightly and let him understand that *I was responsible to my Government and fellow citizens for the handling of the British forces.*"[26] It was a true turning point in Haig's career. From this point on he would command his own battles, with only limited direction from Foch, and from this point on he would prosecute a series of battles on the operational level.

During the coming string of British and Allied successes against German defenders in France and Flanders, much has been made of the fact that only a perceived collapse of German morale allowed the Allied victory. Certainly the German divisions of 1918 were bloodied and tired, but so were those of the BEF. The historical team of Robin Prior and Trevor Wilson dealt with the question of morale in their groundbreaking *Command on the Western Front*, concluding:

In any case, explaining victory and defeat at Amiens in terms of morale misses the real nature of the transaction. High morale could avail German artillerymen little when assailed by such an onslaught of high explosive as delivered by the British counter-battery program, or help German machine-gunners when set upon by a combination of tanks, mortars and rifle grenades in the aftermath of a creeping barrage. . . . The conclusion is inescapable. The Germans, however parlous their circumstances, were defeated by superior firepower tactics, which even their best troops could not withstand.[27]

In offensive operations from August 21 to 23, the Third Army, under the command of General Sir Julian Byng, enjoyed far less numerical superiority and also did not achieve an appreciable level of surprise. More cautious than Rawlinson, Byng moved forward into the Battle of Albert rather slowly, earning Haig's ire, but achieving great results. The shift in attack frontage had somewhat wrongfooted the Germans and helped to break their system of defenses in the area, resulting in the capture of over ten thousand prisoners. The achievement, somewhat less expected than the gains made at Amiens, sparked Haig to believe that the Great War was indeed nearing an end. As a result Haig instructed his army commanders:

> The methods which we have followed, hitherto, in our battles with limited objectives when the enemy was strong, are no longer suited to his present condition.
>
> The enemy has not the means to deliver counter-attacks on an extended scale, nor has he the numbers to hold a position against the very extended advance which is not being directed upon him.
>
> To turn the present situation to account the most resolute offensive is everywhere desirable. Risks which a month ago would have been criminal to incur, ought to be incurred as a duty.[28]

Though both Ludendorff and the Kaiser agreed with Haig's assessment that Germany had lost the war, Haig's renewed hope for decisive battle remained premature. On August 26, Haig extended the attack frontage even further by opening offensive action on the front of the First Army. Fighting remained bitter, and the Germans did not want to give ground, but were forced to retire to their Winter Line of defenses. Nearly constant British pressure, though, quickly flanked the Germans, forcing a further retirement to the security of the Hindenburg Line. During the confusing engagements of late August and early September, tactical command tended to devolve upon those closer to the scene of the semi-mobile series of battles. Thus, though Haig retained overall command, many of the most important decisions now fell to his capable subordinates, including Lieutenant General Sir John Monash, in command of the Australian Corps, and Currie, in command of the Canadian Corps. In all, the great series of victories by the BEF from the Battle of Albert to mid-September had driven the Germans backward over fifteen miles from prepared systems of defense and captured upward of forty thousand prisoners. The cost, though, was heavy at over eighty thousand casualties. The considerable victory was tempered by the fact that the BEF now faced the most formidable defensive network ever constructed on the western front.

Haig remained confident, but was aware that the situation had changed and that immediate, decisive battle no longer seemed possible.[29] In London the British government, while heartened by recent victories, despaired over the ability of the BEF to assail the Hindenburg Line without the battle devolving into another Somme or Third Ypres. Thus Wilson sent Haig a telegram warning the commander in chief that the War Cabinet "would become anxious if we received heavy punishment in attacking the Hindenburg Line without success." The telegram angered Haig, who recorded in his diary:

> The object of this telegram is, no doubt, to save the Prime Minister in case of any failure. So I read it to mean that I can attack the Hindenburg Line if I think it right to do so. The C.I.G.S. and the Cabinet already know that my arrangements are being made to that end. If my attack is successful, I will remain on as C. in C. If we fail, or our losses are excessive, I can hope for no mercy![30]

In early September Haig took his case for a continuation of the offensive directly to the new Secretary of State for War, Lord

Milner. Unconvinced, Milner warned Haig that if he used up British manpower in attacks in 1918, there would be none left, thus compromising Britain's position if the war lingered. After their conversations a worried Milner reported that he "had grave doubts whether he had got inside of D. H.'s head," and that Haig was "ridiculously optimistic." Wilson agreed and argued that the War Cabinet would have to "watch this tendency & stupidity of D. H." Having heard all of the worrisome reports, Lloyd George chose to make an effort to shift British forces away from the western front, allowing the war there to become a rather American affair.[31] However, events in France and Flanders soon proved the Prime Minister wrong and preempted his planning.

Obviously success on the battlefield had done little to ease strained relations between the War Cabinet and the commander in chief of the BEF. However, Haig was fairly free to move forward in his planning, being insulated by Foch's position as the Supreme Commander. In a mark of true coalition warfare the two began to lay plans for a general offensive designed to conclude the war, calling for a French and American assault in the south between the Meuse River and Reims on September 26, followed the next two days by an attack by the British First and Third Armies, and an offensive by the Group of Armies in Flanders (GAF) respectively. The attacks were designed to lock German reserves in place and support the final and most important offensive, undertaken by the British Fourth Army in the center of the line against the strongest part of the German defensive network.

On September 26, American and French forces launched their Meuse-Argonne offensive. Though the attack initially achieved only limited success, it held considerable German forces in the threatened and strategically important area. Further north, facing the formidable defenses of the Canal du Nord, the British Third Army attacked on September 27, and, led by the Canadian Corps, in two days of fighting drove a wedge twelve miles wide and six miles deep into the German defenses, capturing some ten thousand prisoners in the process. The next day the GAF struck in Flanders and drove nearly six miles into the German lines there, very nearly reaching the critical rail hub of Roulers. The losses were indeed so severe that Ludendorff called a meeting with the Kaiser to advise that Germany immediately seek an armistice. However, the worst was yet to come.

Rawlinson's Fourth Army faced the most formidable portion of the Hindenburg Line, a system ranging up to 6,000 yards in depth and numbering six main defensive lines, incorporating the considerable obstacle of the St. Quentin Canal. Attacking and defending forces, roughly equal in number, were both bloodied and exhausted, many having fought for weeks on end without respite. Against the mighty German defenses, Rawlinson could rely only on artillery fire equal in weight to the bombardment that had preceded the disastrous first day on the Somme. Yet both Rawlinson and Haig were confident in the plan of battle, partially developed by Monash. The Fourth Army had not ignored the lessons of years of battle—for the artillery was now so accurate and lethal, and called upon to do so much less, that the weight of shell proved more than enough to complete the task. Much had changed in just over two years' time.

In confused operations on the northern portion of the front, where the St. Quentin Canal ran through a massive tunnel, the attack undertaken by American and Australian forces achieved little, demonstrating that the BEF was still far from perfect. However, further south troops of the Forty-sixth Division, using life belts and small boats to cross the canal, had moved forward 6,000 yards, nearly breaking through the mightiest German defenses on the western front in a single day. In the following week the Fourth Army consolidated its uneven gains and finally pierced the last lines of the central Hindenburg system, breaking out into open ground beyond, having achieved one of the greatest feats of arms in British military history.[32]

Though over a month of hard fighting remained, the fall of the Hindenburg Line spelled Germany's doom in the Great War. As Allied advances continued, Haig began to be concerned with issues beyond the immediate battlefield, for on October 6, the Germans asked for an armistice. Haig was disturbed to learn that Foch demanded what amounted to an unconditional surrender. Though the German army was in full retreat and Germany itself was near disintegration, Haig, seemingly the eternal optimist, now counseled caution. He believed that the Germans were ready to end the war, but also that they could fight on if pressed. When on October 19 Lloyd George asked his opinion concerning armistice terms, Haig replied:

> The German Army is capable of retiring to its own frontier, and holding that line if there should be any attempt to touch the *honour* of the German people and make them fight with the courage of despair. . . . The French and American Armies are not capable of making a serious offensive *now*. The British alone might bring the enemy to his knees. But why expend more British lives—and for what? . . . I therefore advise that we only ask in the armistice for what we intend to hold, and that we set our faces against the French entering Germany to pay off old scores.[33]

While talks regarding a possible armistice continued, the BEF pressed forward, hitting the Germans hard in late October and early November in the Battle of the Selle and the Battle of the Sambre. Though the Germans fought spirited rearguard actions, the advances of the BEF were now coming with greater ease as the German will to fight slowly diminished. As victory became more and more certain, Haig turned his attention increasingly to the coming peace. A voice of reason amid a growing chorus in favor of revenge, Haig was astonished at the growing magnitude of French demands regarding the peace. Fearing that such harsh demands would cause a societal breakdown in Germany on November 1, Haig shared his prescient forebodings concerning the peace with his wife:

> The Peace of the World, for the next 50 years at least, may depend upon the decisions taken! So it is important that our Statesmen should think over the situation carefully and not attempt to so humiliate Germany as to produce the desire for revenge in years to come.[34]

Events, though, moved more quickly than Haig expected. On November 9, the Kaiser abdicated and two days later the Great War came to a rather unexpected end. During 1918 the BEF had come of age and won the greatest victory ever in British history—a victory achieved by an army commanded and led by Field Marshal Sir Douglas Haig. The BEF had faced the brunt of the German offensives in the spring, and, though it had made mistakes and suffered greatly, persevered. During the period of the Hundred Days battles, beginning with Amiens, the BEF had played the most substantial role in an Allied effort that drove the German army and nation to sue for peace. Using superior all-arms coordination the BEF had developed into a "weapons system" capable of defeating the vaunted German army and punching through even the powerful Hindenburg Line in a single day. In all during the period of the Allied offensive the BEF had advanced over one hundred miles, through the strongest defenses on the western front, and captured over 186,000 prisoners. The cost of victory was admittedly high, with the BEF suffering 67,000 fatalities and some 33,000 missing or prisoners, while inflicting losses at least as dire upon the Germans.[35]

As the BEF had come of age in 1918, in many ways so had Haig. Though he had played less of a tactical role in the campaign as it became more mobile, Haig remained in strategic control of a military force that no longer needed his direct guidance, which is in itself a testimony to his success as a commander in chief. Often the recipient of more praise by historians, Ludendorff had squandered the gains made through use of superior tactics by pressing attacks in vain after their chance of strategic success had passed—problems ascribed to Haig in 1916 and 1917. The BEF, though, no longer attempted advances to great depth, but under Haig's direction broadened the scope of their operations to bring pressure on the entire German front. Thus, when combined with the tactical skill gained in years of combat, the strategy instituted by Haig proved to be superior to that of the Germans and was the critical element that brought about Allied victory in 1918.

Haig remained quite taciturn as the war came to an end, only noting in his diary on November 11 simply that, "The Armistice came into force at 11 A.M."[36] To his wife, though, Haig had been rather more candid and reflective regarding the Great War. He wrote, "My first thought is to thank that Power that has guided and guarded me all these anxious years," adding his thanks to his wife for her continued support "to me through these long black days since I left you at Aldershot."[37]

Chapter 7

Conclusion

Even haig's homecoming after the Great War was not without political incident. Lloyd George, who had been conspicuously silent regarding congratulations to Haig and the BEF regarding their roles in the Allied victory, on December 1 hosted a London ceremony in honor of Foch. Haig was slated to ride in the fifth carriage in the procession, along with Henry Wilson, and was not invited to the subsequent reception.[1] Haig recorded in his diary:

> I felt that this was more of an insult than I could put up with, even from the Prime Minister. For the past three years I have effaced myself, because I felt that, to win the war, it was essential that the British and French Armies should get on well together. I have patiently submitted to Lloyd George's conceit and swagger, combined with much boasting as to, 'what *he* had accomplished, thanks to *his* foresight in appointing Foch as C. in C. of the Allied Forces'. . . . The real truth, which history will show, is that the British Army won the war in France in spite of L.G. and I have no intention of taking part in any triumphal ride with Foch, or with any pack of foreigners, through the streets of London, mainly in

order to add to L.G.'s importance and help him in his election campaign.[2]

After this somewhat shabby treatment, Haig received his formal welcome home on December 19, replete with honor guards and presentations at Buckingham Palace. What affected Haig the most about the day, though, was the outpouring of affection from the grateful British people. He recorded that:

> The route was not lined with troops. The reception was essentially a welcome by the people, without any official interference, and I could not help feeling how the cheering from the great masses of all classes came from their hearts. As A.D.C. to King Edward, I have taken part in many functions, but never before have I seen such crowds, or such wholehearted enthusiasm. It was indeed most touching to take part in such a ceremony . . .
>
> To-day, indeed, has been a red letter one in my life. To receive such a spontaneous welcome, all the way from the Coast to my house at Kingston Hill shows how the people of England realise what has been accomplished by the Army and myself. This more than compensates me for the difficulties so often put in my way during hostilities and the coldness displayed towards me by the Prime Minister since the Armistice.[3]

There also remained the delicate but traditional political aspect of rewarding Haig for his wartime service to the nation. In late November Haig had been offered a viscountcy, which he rejected, stating:

> Any question of reward for me may stand over until the P.M. has fixed allowances for Disabled Officers and men as well as . . . for all ranks of the Armies under my orders. I also note that when F.M. French was recalled from the command of the Armies in France for incompetence, he was made a Viscount![4]

During the war Haig had repeatedly expressed his displeasure with the fact that disabled veterans often returned home to live in poverty and had to rely on charity rather than organized state aid. His dedication to the men who had served under his command remained central to Haig's thinking and actions after the war. For nearly three months Haig refused to accept any peerage or monetary reward for his service, rather publicly embarrassing the government into giving quick consideration to the pension needs of disabled British soldiers. When the government responded that the soldiers were being well looked after by the charities, an angered Haig responded, "Officers and their wives . . . will not, and ought not to be asked to, accept *Charity*."

Eventually, though, Haig accepted his reward but only after, "The Govt. has promised to do its duty in the matter—indeed the whole country is now behind me in its determination to see that these gallant fellows and their dependents are properly treated." On August 6, 1919, Haig was granted a pension of 100,000 pounds and was shortly thereafter created an earl. In 1921, the grateful nation also presented Haig with the ancestral home at Bemersyde.[5]

After a brief stay at home Haig returned to the continent, this time to oversee the BEF as it made ready to demobilize from war. What concerned him in the process was a policy known as "pivotalism" through which men who had guaranteed jobs in industry were demobilized first regardless of when they had joined the military. Haig thought the process unfair to those who had served longer and proposed demobilization by complete formations. The government ignored his advice and a serious riot developed at Calais in January when solders returning from leave refused to rejoin their units. Though the riots died down with little fanfare, Churchill, who had taken over the War Office, later remarked; "It is surprising that the Commander-in-Chief's prescient warnings [regarding pivotalism] were utterly ignored, and the Army left to be irritated and almost convulsed by a complicated artificial system open at every point to suspicion of jobbery and humbug."

In April 1919, Haig left the BEF to take command of the Home Forces in Britain, a position he would hold until its abolition in 1920. Haig was not asked to take part in the peace process, nor would he have thought his participation in that process to be proper. Again Churchill commented on the situation:

Early in 1919 . . . Lord Haig walked ashore at Dover after the total defeat of Germany and disappeared into private life. . . . Titles, grants, honours of every kind, all the symbols of public gratitude were showered upon him; but he was given no work. He did not join the counsels of the nation; he was not invited to reorganize its army; he was not consulted upon the Treaties; no sphere of public activity was opened to him.[6]

Haig, though, remained quite busy and devoted his life to championing the cause of the soldiers who had served under his command in the Great War. Chief in this regard was Haig's tireless work with the British Legion. In the wake of the war several veterans' organizations had sprung into being, organizations that were often at odds with one another. Haig used his considerable fame, though, to press for unity between the various organizations so that veterans of the Great War could speak with one voice. Haig was also quite passionate in his belief that the organization should foster unity through the inclusion of veterans of all ranks. Thus, though Haig did not create the British Legion, his support and guidance was critical to its foundation.[7]

Haig would serve as the President of the British Legion from its foundation in 1921 until his death in 1928. During the time period Haig worked hard to keep the Legion from becoming a political instrument of discord. Mainly, though, he devoted his seemingly tireless energy to the welfare of his ex-soldiers. As such Haig was in high demand for making speeches at Legion functions, including the unveilings of monuments across the length and breadth of Britain as the nation came to terms with the losses it had suffered in the Great War. On such occasions Haig spoke of his men in glowing and rather fatherly terms. Accepting the Freedom of the City of Stirling in October 1922 Haig remarked:

> More than all else, perhaps, I am pleased to think that I am to meet a gathering of ex-servicemen this afternoon. I am glad to think that I am looked on not only as their old commander, but as a comrade and a friend. I owe too much to the gallant men of all ranks who served with me in France to forget them now, or, as far as I can prevent it, to allow others to forget them.[8]

Haig's sense of duty and paternalism drove him to honor and champion his men. In so doing he stood nearly alone among the commanders of the Great War. Veterans' movements in France and Germany were bitterly divided by politics and served as catalysts for social unrest and political violence. That Haig played a pivotal role in the foundation of the British Legion, which fought for the rights of veterans within the existing political and social system, can be seen as one of Haig's most important achievements.[9]

While others involved in the Great War worked on their autobiographies, heralding the "War Book Boom" of the 1930s and opening the heated debate on the nature of the conflict, Haig again remained, in the main, aloof from the fray—allowing his conduct of the war to speak for itself. He even insisted that a glowing report on his command, to be published by Kiggell, not be released until 1940.[10] Seemingly above sordid conflict, and constant in his desire to champion the cause of those who had served in World War I, Haig quickly became revered throughout Britain. Though he had been a rather distant figure as commander in chief, in peacetime Haig was now very much a beloved father figure to veterans of the Great War.

Haig continued to toil in the veterans' movement, even to the point of physical exhaustion. Until the very end he continued faithfully to answer all correspondence in his own hand, without the aid of a secretary. Toward the end of his life his doctors warned him to lighten his work load, but he refused.[11] Haig died unexpectedly on the evening of January 29, 1928, at the age of sixty-seven. In elaborate funeral arrangements, Haig lay in state both in London and in Edinburgh. In London an estimated 25,000 people filed by his coffin each day, and later in Edinburgh crowds of similar size packed the sidewalks for miles in freezing sleet waiting to pay their respects. Across the nation, those who could not participate in the ceremony listened as the BBC made the memorial service one of its first ever live broadcasts.

The spontaneous outpouring of affection for Haig upon his death was of a magnitude reserved only for heroes of great national importance, equaling the grief expressed at the time of the death of perhaps Britain's best loved leader, Sir Winston Churchill, some thirty-five years later.[12] Haig's hero status seemed well deserved. He had taken over the command of a faltering BEF and had fought doggedly on through the trials and tribulations of the Somme and Passchendaele. Though everyone in Britain mourned the losses of those battles, they were not yet perceived to be fruitless disasters, but costly victories. Britain still stood in the relative afterglow of success, and thus to most Britons in 1928 Haig remained the commander in chief who had won Britain's greatest ever military victory—an achievement as yet unclouded by the coming of the Second World War. Future generations of historians, though, would come to question the wisdom and judgment of the crowds of 1928 and speculate on the nature of Haig's achievement, allowing the Great War to continue in another guise. Though the historical trench warfare concerning his tenure as commander in chief will continue, Haig was neither the savior of Britain nor the butcher of the BEF. Haig was indeed a product of his time, an Edwardian gentleman officer confronted by the horrors of the first truly modern war. Though he made mistakes and learned slowly, Haig did learn, and more quickly than the military leaders of the other combatant nations. Suffering through years of travail, the BEF, under Haig's leadership, was transformed into a modern force that in many ways redefined warfare and was capable of defeating the vaunted Germans. Thus, after the passage of nearly eighty years and after numerous acrimonious historical debates, the assessment of Haig's command has come full circle, for the wisdom and judgment of the crowds of 1928 seems right and proper after all.

Notes

Preface
1. Brian Bond, "The Somme in British History," in Geoffrey Jensen and Andrew Wiest, eds., *War in the Age of Technology* (New York: New York University Press, 2001).
2. Daniel Todman, "'Sans peur et sans reproche': The Retirement, Death and Mourning of Sir Douglas Haig, 1918–1928." *The Journal of Military History* (October 2003, Vol. 67. No. 4), 1088.
3. J. M. Bourne, "Haig and the Historians," in Brian Bond and Nigel Cave, eds., *Haig: A Reappraisal 70 Years On.* (London: Leo Cooper, 1999), 1.
4. Denis Winter, *Haig's Command* (London: Viking, 1991). For treatments of Haig and his place in history see, J. M. Bourne, "Haig and the Historians," in Brian Bond and Nigel Cave, eds., *Haig: A Reappraisal 70 Years On* (London: Leo Cooper, 1999), and Keith Simpson, "The Reputation of Sir Douglas Haig," in Brian Bond, ed., *The First World War and British Military History* (London: Clarendon, 1991).
5. Gary Sheffield, *Forgotten Victory* (London: Headline, 2001), 135.
6. Robin Prior and Trevor Wilson, "Review of Denis Winter, *Haig's Command: A Reassessment*," *Australian War Memorial Journal* (23, October 1993), 57.

Chapter 1
1. John Charteris, *Field-Marshal Earl Haig* (New York: Charles Scribner's Sons, 1929), 4.
2. Gerard J. De Groot, *Douglas Haig, 1861–1928* (London: Unwin Hyman, 1989), 18–23.
3. Ibid., 27.

4.   Gerard J. De Groot, "Ambition, Duty and Doctrine: Douglas Haig's Rise to High Command," in Bond, *Haig: A Reappraisal,* 42–48.

5.   Tim Travers, *The Killing Ground* (London: Unwin Hyman, 1987).

6.   De Groot, "Ambition, Duty and Doctrine," in Bond, *Haig: A Reappraisal,* 41.

7.   De Groot, *Haig,* 59.

8.   Ian F. W. Beckett, "Haig and French," in Bond, *Haig: A Reappraisal,* 55, and Richard Holmes, "The Last Hurrah: Cavalry on the Western Front, August to September 1914," in Hugh Cecil and Peter Liddle, eds., *Facing Armageddon: The First World War Experienced* (London: Leo Cooper, 1996), 288.

9.   Ibid., 41–42; Charteris, *Haig,* 32–33.

10. Terraine, *Haig,* 40.

11. Charteris, *Haig,* 55–56.

12. Denis Winter, *Haig's Command: A Reassessment* (New York: Viking, 1991) 13.

Chapter 2

1.   Gerald French, *The Life of Field-Marshal Sir John French* (London: Cassell, 1931), 237. Also see Andrew Wiest, *Passchendaele and the Royal Navy* (Westport: Greenwood Press, 1995).

2.   Robert Blake, ed., *The Private Papers of Douglas Haig, 1914–1919.* (London: Eyre & Spottiswoode, 1952), Haig diary entry, August 5, 1914.

3.   For a summary of the French-Kitchener relationship see Richard Holmes, "Sir John French and Lord Kitchener," in Bond, *The First World War.*

4.   Blake, *Papers,* Haig diary entry, August 11, 1914.

5.   Ibid., Haig diary entry, August 13, 1914.

6.   Holmes, "French and Kitchener," in Bond, *The First World War,* 120.

7.   De Groot, *Haig,* 159.

8.   Ibid., 162.

9.   Terraine, *Haig,* 93–94.

10. Wiest, *Passchendaele,* 3–9.

11. Terraine, *Haig,* 102–103.

12. De Groot, *Haig*, 166.

13. Ibid., 168.

Chapter 3

1. Robin Prior and Trevor Wilson, *Command on the Western Front* (Oxford: Blackwell, 1992), 36–38.

2. For a summary of communications advances see Paddy Griffith, *Battle Tactics of the Western Front: The British Army's Art of Attack, 1916–1918* (New Haven: Yale, 1994), 169–175.

3. Andy Wiest, *The Illustrated History of World War I* (London: Brown Books, 2001), 73.

4. Shelford Bidwell and Dominick Graham, *Fire-Power: British Army Weapons and Theories of War, 1904–1945* (Boston: Allen & Unwin, 1982), 62–65; De Groot, *Haig*, 27–53.

5. Wiest, *Passchendaele*, 20–26; War Council Minutes, January 1915, Cabinet Papers, CAB 22/1, British National Archives, Kew.

6. Haig Diary, entry for February 25, 1915, British National Archives, Kew.

7. Prior and Wilson, *Command*, 31.

8. Ibid., 44–51.

9. Ibid., 78.

10. De Groot, *Haig*, 183; Bidwell and Graham, *Fire-Power*, 75.

11. Prior and Wilson, *Command*, 83.

12. Ibid., 85.

13. Blake, *Papers*, 93, Haig diary entry, May 11, 1915.

14. Terraine, *Haig*, 148–149.

15. Holmes, "Sir John French," in Bond, *The First World War*, 125–128.

16. Blake, *Papers*, Haig diary entry, August 7, 1915, and August 19, 1915.

17. Prior and Wilson, *Command*, 108–112.

18. Terraine, *Haig*, 157.

19. De Groot, *Haig*, 207.

20. Blake, *Papers*, Haig diary entry, October 24, 1915.

21. Griffith, *Battle Tactics*, 53.

Chapter 4

1. John Hussey, "Portrait of a Commander-in-Chief," in Bond, *Haig*, 19.

2. See Gary Sheffield, "The Morale of the British Army on the Western Front, 1914–1918," in Jensen and Wiest, *War in the Age of Technology*, 105–139.

3. Blake, *Papers*, Haig diary entry, March 29, 1916.

4. Prior and Wilson, *Command*, 138.

5. De Groot, *Haig*, 220.

6. Terraine, *Haig*, 176.

7. Ibid., 173. Also see Nigel Cave, "Haig and Religion," in Bond, *Haig*, 240–260; and G. S. Duncan, *Douglas Haig As I Knew Him* (London: Allen and Unwin, 1966).

8. Hussey, "Portrait," in Bond, *Haig*, 20.

9. Peter Simkins, "Haig and the Army Commanders," in Bond, *Haig*, 94–95.

10. De Groot, *Haig*, 223.

11. David R. Woodward, "Sir William Robertson and Sir Douglas Haig," in Bond, *Haig*, 65–67; also see David R. Woodward, *Field Marshal Sir William Robertson Chief of the Imperial General Staff in the Great War* (Westport: Greenwood, 1998).

12. Haig Diary, entry for December 28, 1915.

13. Ibid., December 21, 1915.

14. Blake, *Papers*, Haig diary entry, June 7, 1916.

15. Gary Sheffield, *The Somme* (London: Cassell, 2003), 25.

16. Prior and Wilson, *Command*, 141.

17. Ibid., 169.

18. Haig Diary, entry for June 30, 1916.

19. Sheffield, *Somme*, 50.

20. Fricourt actually fell on the next day, due to British advances on its flanks making the defensive works there untenable.

21. Prior and Wilson, *Command*, 184.

22. Sheffield, *Somme*, 68.

23. Blake, *Papers*, Haig diary entry, July 3, 1916.

24. Prior and Wilson, *Command*, 187–193.

25. Gary Sheffield, *Forgotten Victory: The First World War: Myths and Realities* (London: Headline, 2001), 173–174.

26. Blake, Papers, Note on letter received from CIGS dated July 29.

27. Prior and Wilson, *Command*, 203–205.

28. Ibid., 230.

29. J. P. Harris, "Haig and The Tank," in Bond, *Haig*, 146–147.

30. De Groot, *Haig*, 265–266.

31. Terraine, *Haig*, 222.

32. David Lloyd George, *War Memoirs* (London: Odhams, 1938), 385.

33. Harris, "Haig and The Tank," in Bond, *Haig*, 148–149. One of the best recent accounts of the tank's development and use can be found in J. P. Harris, *Men Ideas and Tanks* (Manchester: Manchester University Press, 1995).

34. John Laffin, *British Butchers and Bunglers of World War One* (Wolfeboro Falls, NH: Sutton, 1988), 99.

35. E. Ludendorff, *My War Memories, 1914–1918* (London: Hutchinson, n.d.), 307.

36. Sheffield, *Somme*, 162.

Chapter 5

1. "Report on Naval Affairs, October 1916," November 2, 1916, Cabinet Papers, CAB 22/62.

2. H. H. Asquith, A Note to Robertson, November 21, 1916, Cabinet Papers, CAB 22/70.

3. De Groot, *Haig*, 227.

4. De Groot, *Haig*, 288.

5. Sir Maurice Hankey, *The Supreme Command* (London: Allen and Unwin, 1961), 2:616–617.

6. Haig Diary, entry for February 26, 1917.

7. Robin Prior and Trevor Wilson, *Passchendaele: The Untold Story* (New Haven: Yale University Press, 1996), 29, 55–56.

8. Wiest, *Passchendaele*, 77.

9. "Preliminary Report on Proposed Operations in the Nieuport Sector," Sir Henry Rawlinson Papers, Fourth Army Records, 19:102, Imperial War Musuem.

10. Kiggell to Plumer and Gough, May 24 and 29, 1917, War Office Papers, WO 158/215, British National Archives, Kew.

11. Haig to Robertson, June 12, 1917, Cabinet Papers, CAB 27/7, wp 3.

12. Blake, *Papers*, Robertson to Haig, June 13, 1917.

13. For a full discussion of the effect of the Admiralty on the planning of the Third Battle of Ypres, see Wiest, *Passchendaele*.

14. See Travers, *Killing Ground*.

15. For a fuller discussion of the planning of Third Ypres see Andrew Wiest, "Haig, Gough and Passchendaele," in Gary

Sheffield, ed., *Leadership and Command: The Anglo-American Experience Since 1861* (London: Brassey's, 1997).

16. Gough to Edmonds, February 2, 1944, Cabinet Papers, CAB 45/140.

17. Prior and Wilson, *Passchendaele*, 82–84.

18. Kiggell to Army Commanders, August 7, 1917, Haig Papers, Acc. 3155 (116), National Library of Scotland.

19. Prior and Wilson, *Passchendaele*, 114–116.

20. Ibid., 134.

21. See Heinz Hagenluke, "The German High Command," and German Werth, "Flanders 1917 and the German Soldier," in Peter H. Liddle, ed., *Passchendaele in Perspective* (London: Leo Cooper, 1997).

22. Wiest, *Passchendaele*, 167.

23. J. E. Edmonds, *Official History of the War, Military Operations, France and Belgium, 1917* (London: Macmillian, 1948), 2:iv.

24. For a more complete and controversial look at Cambrai planning see Harris, *Men Ideas and Tanks*.

25. Harris, *Men Ideas and Tanks*, 125.

26. Terraine, *Haig*, 379.

27. Prior and Wilson, *Passchendaele*, 155.

28. Blake, *Papers*, Robertson to Haig December 6, 1917.

Chapter 6

1. David Woodward, *Lloyd George and the Generals* (Newark: University of Delaware Press, 1983), 221.

2. Terraine, *Haig*, 385, Derby to Haig, December 7, 1917.

3. De Groot, *Haig*, 354, Haig to Derby, December 10, 1917.

4. Blake, *Papers*, Haig diary entry, January 12, 1918.

5. Woodward, *Lloyd George*, 236, Lloyd George to Esher, December 1, 1917. It is important to note that while Lloyd George did use manpower as a tool of control, recent research suggests that the defeats suffered by the British in the coming German offensive were not due to Lloyd George starving the military of strength. For a detailed account of the controversy see Woodward, *Lloyd George*, chapters 10 and 11.

6. De Groot, *Haig*, 363.

7. Blake, *Papers*, Haig diary entries, February 10 and 11, 1918.

8. De Groot, *Haig*, 368, Haig diary entry, March 10, 1918.

9. Woodward, *Lloyd George*, 278.

10. Terraine, *Haig*, 391, 400.

11. Ibid., 396.

12. De Groot, *Haig*, 367.

13. Terraine, *Haig*, 409, Instructions to the Fifth Army, February 9, 1918.

14. Blake, *Papers*, 290, Haig to Lady Haig, February 28, 1918.

15. Woodward, *Lloyd George*, 285.

16. Blake, *Papers*, Haig diary entries, March 23 and 24, 1918.

17. Ibid., 298, Haig diary entry, March 26, 1918.

18. For the operational weaknesses of the German system of attack in 1918 see Sheffield, *Forgotten Victory*, 230–231.

19. Terraine, *Haig*, 432–433.

20. De Groot, *Haig*, 379.

21. Blake, *Papers*, 308, Haig to Lady Haig, May 7, 1918.

22. Prior and Wilson, *Command*, 305.

23. Ibid., 306–314.

24. J. P. Harris, *Amiens to the Armistice: The BEF in the Hundred Days' Campaign, 8 August-11 November, 1918* (London: Brassey's, 1998); 103–107.

25. Blake, *Papers*, 322, Haig diary entry, August 8, 1918.

26. Ibid., Haig diary entry, August 14, 1918.

27. Prior and Wilson, *Command*, 320.

28. Harris, *Amiens to the Armistice*, 145, Haig to Army Commanders, August 22, 1918.

29. Ibid., 167.

30. Blake, *Papers*, Haig diary entry, August 29, 1918.

31. Woodward, *Lloyd George*, 333.

32. Prior and Wilson, *Command*, 369–374; Harris, *Amiens to the Armistice*, 218–225.

33. Ibid., 333–334, Haig diary entry, October 19, 1918.

34. De Groot, *Haig*, 394, Haig to Lady Haig, November 1, 1918.

35. Harris, *Amiens to the Armistice*, 295.

36. Blake, *Papers*, Haig diary entry, November 11, 1918.

37. De Groot, *Haig*, Haig to Lady Haig, November 9, 1918.

Chapter 7

1. De Groot, *Haig*, 397.

2. Blake, *Papers*, Haig diary entry, November 30, 1918.

3. Ibid., Haig diary entry, December 19, 1918.

4. Ibid., Haig diary entry, November 19, 1918.

5. De Groot, *Haig*, 399–400.

6. Terraine, *Haig*, 483–484.

7. Niall Barr and Gary Sheffield, "Douglas Haig, the Common Soldier, and the British Legion," in Bond, *Haig*, 229–230.

8. Todman, "*Sans peur et sans reproche*," 1095.

9. Barr and Sheffield, "Douglas Haig, the Common Soldier, and the British Legion," 232.

10. De Groot, *Haig*, 406. Haig, though, took an indirect role in the debate by aiding in Boraston and Dewar's publication of his Dispatches.

11. Ibid., 404.

12. Todman, "*Sans peur et sans reproche*," 1088.

Bibliographic Note

SOURCE MATERIAL regarding Haig and his role in the Great War is abundant and ranges from a myriad of important secondary works to plentiful archival sources located across the United Kingdom. Any serious research into Haig's career, though, must start with the use of his voluminous diary and personal papers located in the National Library of Scotland and copied in the British National Archives (formerly known as the Public Record Office) in Kew. Further evidence can be found in the massive collection of War Office documents in the National Archives and in the papers of his subordinates and colleagues, including those of General Sir Henry Rawlinson at the Churchill College Archives in Cambridge and those of both General Sir Launcelot Kiggell and Field Marshal Sir William Robertson at the Liddell Hart Centre for Military Archives in London. Though the present study relies on extensive research in these and several other collections, footnotes were kept to a minimum for the sake of readability. The study is meant to serve as an introduction to the field and to the man, rather than as an exhaustive new archival biography. It is the author's hope that this volume will whet the appetite of a new audience, introducing them to the oft-ignored gold mine that is the present history of the Great War.

There are several important books on Haig, ranging from hagiographic biographies written by contemporaries to quite damning more recent accounts of his career. The following list is by no means complete, but again serves as an introduction to the ongoing argument concerning Haig's tenure as commander in chief of the BEF. A most valuable source is Robert Blake's edited version of Haig's diaries and papers, *The Private Papers of Douglas Haig, 1914–1919*. (London: Eyre & Spottiswoode, 1952). Though of great importance to understanding the topic, Blake's work leaves much to be desired. At present Dr. Gary Sheffield is working on a new and fuller edited version of Haig's papers, which will prove to be a critical resource. John Charteris's *Field-Marshal Earl Haig* (New York: Charles Scribner's Sons, 1929) and George Dewar's *Sir Douglas Haig's Command* (Boston: Houghton Mifflin, 1923) are good starting points for a sympathetic view of Haig in the immediate postwar period.

Recently the traditionalist school of thought has been represented by Denis Winter, *Haig's Command: A Reassessment* (New York: Viking, 1991), a deeply flawed volume that takes Haig to task on a myriad of issues, and Gerard J. De Groot's valuable and well-researched *Douglas Haig, 1861–1928* (London: Unwin Hyman, 1989). The revisionist school of thought was in many ways founded in John Terraine's landmark *Douglas Haig: The Educated Soldier* (London: Hutchinson, 1963). As arguments about Haig have continued, more recent compilations have appeared that serve to put the historical debate into a truly modern context, including Brian Bond and Nigel Cave's *Haig: A Reappraisal 70 Years On* (London: Leo Cooper, 1999).

Haig also features as a central figure in most of the broader accounts of the Great War. In the past thirty years the historiography of World War I has flowered and come of age as the arguments about the nature of the war continue. Though there are far too many books on the subject to list here, what follows is a good starting point for further research. Tim Travers's *The Killing Ground* (London: Unwin Hyman, 1987), and *How the War Was Won* (New York: Routledge, 1992) are important to understanding how Haig's military training interacted with the reality of the Great War. Shelford Bidwell and Dominick Graham's *Fire-Power: British Army Weapons and Theories of War, 1904–1945* (Boston: Allen & Unwin, 1982), is an unsurpassed survey of the use of firepower in World War I. Robin Prior and Trevor Wilson's *Command on the Western Front* (Oxford: Blackwell, 1992), chronicles the career of General Sir Henry Rawlinson and also serves as a very important documentation of the BEF's ongoing learning curve. Finally, two of the more valuable general works that put the revisionist views of the Great War into perspective are Gary Sheffield's *Forgotten Victory: The First World War: Myths and Realities* (London: Headline, 2001), and Paddy Griffith, *Battle Tactics of the Western Front: The British Army's Art of Attack, 1916–1918* (New Haven: Yale, 1994).

There are several books on more specific subjects, ranging from individual battles to accounts of political infighting, that are important to a full understanding of Haig's career. Many accounts of the Somme exist and those interested in further reading on the battle can begin their pursuit with Martin Middlebrook, *The First Day on the Somme* (New York: Penguin, 1971); Gary Sheffield, *The Somme* (London: Cassell, 2003); Malcolm Brown, *The Imperial War Museum Book of the Somme* (London: Sidgwick & Jackson, 1996); and Michael Chappell, *The Somme 1916: Crucible of a British Army* (London: Crowood Press, 1995). Relatively few books deal exclusively with the Third Battle of Ypres. However, for further reading and inquiry see Leon Wolff, *In Flanders Fields* (London: Longmans, 1960); Andrew Wiest, *Passchendaele and the Royal Navy* (Westport: Greenwood, 1995); Robin Prior and Trevor Wilson, *Passchendaele: The Untold Story* (New Haven: Yale University Press, 1996); Peter H. Liddle, ed., *Passchendaele in Perspective* (London: Leo Cooper, 1997); and Nigel Steel and Peter Hart, *Passchendaele: The Sacrificial Ground* (London: Cassell, 2002). For reading on the German offensives of 1918 and German methods of attack see Martin Middlebrook, *The Kaiser's Battle, 21 March 1918: The First Day of the German Spring Offensive* (London: Allen Lane, 1978); B. I. Gudmunsson, *Stormtroop Tactics: Innovation in the German Army, 1914–1918* (New York: Praeger, 1989); and Holger Herwig, *The First World War: Germany and Austria-Hungary, 1914–1918* (London: Arnold, 1997). For treatments of the Amiens Offensive and British actions during the "Hundred

Days," see J. P. Harris, *Amiens to the Armistice: The BEF in the Hundred Days' Campaign, 8 August–11 November, 1918* (London: Brassey's, 1998); and John Terraine, *To Win a War: 1918 the Year of Victory* (London: Sidgewick and Jackson, 1978).

Finally, there also exists a multitude of books regarding the political turmoil surrounding the course of the war. The most important primary sources include: David Lloyd George, *War Memoirs* (London: Odhams, 1938); Sir William Robertson, *Soldiers and Statesmen* (London: Cassell, 1926); Lord Beaverbrook, *Men and Power* (London: Hutchinson, 1956); Winston Churchill, *The World Crisis* (London: Thornton, 1924); and The Earl of Oxford and Asquith, *Memories and Reflections* (London: Cassell, 1928). Important secondary sources on the matter include: David Woodward, *Lloyd George and the Generals* (Newark: University of Delaware Press, 1983); Bentley Gilbert, *David Lloyd George* (Columbus: Ohio State University, 1987); and Trevor Wilson, *The Myriad Faces of War* (Cambridge: Polity Press, 1986).

About the Author

Andrew A. Wiest is a Professor of History at the University of Southern Mississippi and a former visiting lecturer at the Royal Military Academy, Sandhurst. He co-directs the university's Center for the Study of War and Society and developed and co-directs the university's award-winning Vietnam study abroad program. Presently engaged in research concerning the Vietnam War, his previous published works include *Passchendaele and the Royal Navy* (Greenwood, 1995); *War in the Age of Technology*, co-edited with Geoffrey Jensen (New York University Press, 2001); and *The Vietnam War, 1956–1975* (Osprey, 2002). The author's burgeoning family includes his wife Jill, his two-year-old daughter Abigail, and his new son Luke.

MILITARY PROFILES
AVAILABLE

Farragut: America's First Admiral
Robert J. Schneller, Jr.
Drake: For God, Queen, and Plunder
Wade G. Dudley
Santa Anna: A Curse Upon Mexico
Robert L. Scheina
Eisenhower: Soldier-Statesman of the American Century
Douglas Kinnard
Semmes: Rebel Raider
John M. Taylor
Doolittle: Aerospace Visionary
Dik Alan Daso
Foch: Supreme Allied Commander in the Great War
Michael S. Neiberg
Villa: Soldier of the Mexican Revolution
Robert L. Scheina
Cushing: Civil War SEAL
Robert J. Schneller, Jr.
Alexander the Great: Invincible King of Macedonia
Peter G. Tsouras
Hindenburg: Icon of German Militarism
William J. Astore and Dennis E. Showalter
Franco: Soldier, Commander, Dictator
Geoffrey Jensen
Forrest: The Confederacy's Relentless Warrior
Robert M. Browning, Jr.
Meade: Victor of Gettysburg
Richard A. Sauers

MILITARY PROFILES
FORTHCOMING

Halsey
Robert J. Cressman
Tirpitz
Michael Epkenhans
Petain
Robert B. Bruce
Winfield Scott
Samuel Watson
Benedict Arnold
Mark Hayes